"HE IS A ONE-MAN COMBINATION OF TOUGHNESS, DRIVING AMBITION, ARTISTIC TALENT, MUSICAL SKILL, FEEL FOR MELODY, ACCOMPANIED BY CAUTION, FINANCIAL CUNNING, A PERCEPTION OF HUMAN NATURE, A MEMORY FOR DETAIL (IN CONVERSATION HE WILL DISCUSS INCIDENTS THAT HAPPENED TEN YEARS EARLIER WITH TOTAL RECALL), A DEEP AND ABIDING LOVE FOR HIS FAMILY, A POLITICAL AWARENESS, AND THE NATURAL CHARM OF A DIPLOMAT"

Here is Paul McCartney as the public loves him.

Here is Paul McCartney as heretofore only his most intimate friends and lovers have known him.

Here, at last—frank, true, and totally uncensored, told by a man who himself is prominent in the rock world, is—

THE PAUL McCARTNEY STORY

The Paul McCartney Story

by George Tremlett

POPULAR LIBRARY - TORONTO

ACKNOWLEDGMENT

So much has been written about Paul McCartney that I have chosen a different approach in writing this book to the others in the series. The chronology in the first appendix is expanded to give a day-by-day, year-by-year account of McCartney's career, his relationship with the other Beatles, his private life, his marriage, and his individual work with Wings. And then in the text itself, I have avoided repeating this—and have tried to expand on the different aspects of his life and his work to show how McCartney has developed as a person.

In writing this book I had drawn on my own interviews over a period of twelve years with many people who have been connected with McCartney, sometimes quoting directly, and in others relating material in the third person, from—Paul and Linda McCartney, his brother Mike (McGear), Denny Laine, Nigel Whalley and Ken Brown (who were both original members of The Quarrymen), the late Brian Epstein, the late Rory Storm and his mother, the late Mrs. Vi Caldwell, the other Beatles, John's aunt (Mrs. Mimi Smith), George Harrison's parents Mr. and the late Mrs. Harrison, George's brother Harry, Bill Harry (who was at art school with Lennon and edited *Mersey Beat*), George Martin, Geoff Emerick, and many musicians who have worked with McCartney.

Chapter One

Even now, after all the books and magazine articles, the TV interviews, records and films, very little is really known about Paul McCartney or any of the other Beatles. It is generally assumed that their lives became public property in the mid-Sixties, and that everything they did thereafter was captured by the public prints, but that was never true. Few pressmen got really close to them, even their official biography and their own monthly magazine really gave very little away, and if the image that developed around them was far from true then they themselves did very little to dispel the illusions.

Indeed, one of the strangest features of the whole industry that has developed around rock music is that the myths remain intact. Its stars remain very private people, often extremely skilled in matters of law and high finance, and certainly far shrewder than most City businessmen, newspaper executives and rising politicians of the day. Yet this is the side the public never sees; someone like Paul McCartney will appear in a television interview, engage in polite conversation, smile freely, gently deflect any questions that may come a little too close to avoid talking about such matters as money in anything other than a self-deprecating way, steering around any discussion of deep personal relationships—and the myths retain their glamour.

Yet it would be quite wrong to say that all this is a carefully contrived façade. The explanation is much more simple than that; within the music business there is a convention that certain subjects are never discussed with the press. At one time it was *verboten* to mention wives or girlfriends, and many artists are still reluctant to do so—even now there are many well known performers who are secretly married. Likewise, it is still not considered wise to conduct interviews on too high an intellectual level, and any mention of money is enough to end any conversation. This is an understandable precaution in an industry where it is possible to gross in a week as much as the U.S. President earns in a year (there are only a few artists with earnings at that level, but a great many trying to get there), making it necessary for many top rock stars to be reasonably expert in multi-national company law and taxation. The result of all this is that the stars themselves are in nearly every case totally different people from what their audience thinks they are.

In Paul McCartney's case, he is more sophisticated, more intellectual, more skilled in finance, tougher in business and in his pace of working—and at the same time close to his family, fairly old-fashioned in moral outlook, quite conventional in some of his attitudes, and yet in every sense much more normal than people outside the music business would ever think possible. His manners are exceptional, and yet he drives himself and those around him at such a pace that even members of his present band, Wings, find it hard to keep up with him and tire long before he does. He can be quite ruthless when he feels he has to be.

This is not, I suspect, the image he enjoys with most of those people who followed his career with The Beatles and more recently on his own, with his wife Linda and with Wings, but the truth is that you need to be very level and strong in character to survive in rock music as McCartney has done, for it's now a vast industry, grossing just in British record sales alone some £210,000,000 a year (which is approximately four times the annual box office income of the British film industry), and it is an industry growing so fast world-wide with so many fringe companies selling merchandise, publishing, marketing and collecting other forms of royalties that statistically one can never keep up with it. However, it is still a very small business in terms of people, numbering at its heart in successful musicians, writers, agents, publishers, managers, arrangers and publicists just a few hundred people, linked by contracts and friendship; a coterie as exclusive as any masonic lodge, operating world-wide almost as a separate kingdom—with Paul McCartney as one of its princes.

McCartney's influence on the music of rock has been profound; he more than anyone has widened its appeal to the world outside. Until the Beatles came along, rock music was largely a teenage phenomenon and most parents were frightened by its effect on their children—because they believed from their daily papers that rock 'n' roll was the music of the Teddy Boys, the Hells Angels and the seedy cafes and ballrooms where violence broke out. There were very heavy sexual undertones, too—but once The Beatles arrived all that was largely forgotten. Dressed in their Pierre Cardin suits, wide-eyed and smiling, with their mop tops and quick wit, they reassured the Mums. Of course, that was all another myth if the truth be known. There was nothing saintly about them at all. They boozed and womanised, experimented with pills and drugs, and occasionally even came to blows. But their fans never heard about that. So far as the public were concerned, they were "the boys" who had become as big in their way as Elvis Presley and Frank Sinatra had in theirs. Of them all, Paul McCartney was idolised the most by teenage girls the world over—he was everyone's favourite Beatle.

In fact his influence went much deeper than that—for it was he who first worked with a string quartet (on the hauntingly beautiful "Yesterday"), and who wrote many of the classic Beatle melodies. Another of the myths was that he and John Lennon were always supposed to write together—which in fact they seldom did; most of their songs were largely written by one or the other, and sometimes numbers that only one of them had written would still be credited to them both. It was he who first had his music played by orchestras such as the Boston Symphony Orchestra, who became the first rock musician to work with a brass band (the Black Dyke Mills Band when recording "Thingumybob"), who became the first rock musician to move into film music with his sound-track for the Hayley Mills film "The Family Way" (and if you doubt the lasting quality of his work just listen to that score again), who first recorded Mary Hopkin, who launched Badfinger with their first hit, and who has worked successfully with musicians ranging from the semi-folk of Silkie to the traditional jazz of Chris Barber or the rhythm 'n' blues based music of Cliff Bennett. Now in recent years he has moved on yet again with his own band Wings recording two of the most successful albums of the Seventies "Red Rose Speedway" and "Band On The Run."

Financially, all this has made him a millionaire many times over—for remember that every time you hear a Paul McCartney song (or a Beatles song that he helped to write) on radio, television or in a dancehall, on a juke box, or at a concert (whether played by him or by somebody else), a royalty will afterwards find its way back to McCartney's network of companies. And when you read of the millions of pounds made in profits by the original Beatles song publishing company Northern Songs (now part of ATV), remember that those profits were only made in handling *half* of the Lennon-McCartney songwriting income—the other fifty percent goes straight back to the songwriter under the traditional copublishing arrangements within the music business. And when you read that The Beatles earned £17,500,000 in eight and a half years, remember that that figure did *not* include the songwriting income of Paul McCartney and John Lennon.

It is his music that is the primary source of Paul McCartney's vast private fortune. Just take the one song "Yesterday"—within eighteen months of that song first being recorded more than forty artistes had all recorded just that one song. And that was only the start of the "Yesterday" story; for within just those eighteen months no fewer than 400—yes, FOUR HUNDRED—other versions of that one song were recorded around the world. And every time each of those artistes sang or performed that song, every time their version was played on radio or TV, another royalty found its way back to Paul McCartney, who had originally called it "Scrambled Eggs" because he could not think of a better title.

Had you written just that one song, you could have retired your parents and set up home in Switzerland—and never worked again. But McCartney has never stopped. Many of the songs that were originally published in the joint names of him and John Lennon—classic numbers like "All My Loving," "Here, There and Everywhere," "Eleanor Rigby," "Yellow Submarine," "Michelle," "And I Love Her," "I Saw Her Standing There" etc. have been covered hundreds of times. Every time a record buyer goes into his local store and buys one of those cover versions (whether it be on a single or as an album track); every time one of those cover versions is played on radio or a juke box, and every time one of those artistes appears in concert and sings the number live, another royalty goes back to the songwriters.

Of course, the taxman gets his share; some royalties that should have accrued may disappear because a recording company in a far-off country goes bankrupt or because a tiny dance band playing at village hops fails to make its return to the Performing Rights Society, but with so vast a basic income as this it is possible for someone in Paul McCartney's position to arrange his affairs in such a way that their wealth just grows and grows and grows.

It means they have to be prudent, but McCartney has never been a fool with his money—and his father-in-law and brother-in-law are partners in one of the world's leading firms of show business lawyers. McCartney himself is decisive and forthright, sometimes hesitating before an important decision—but sticking to that decision once made. It is an attitude that permeates every area of his life. He was the first of The Beatles to make sure that his father was secure financially (for which there were strong family reasons; Paul's mother had died when he was in his teens and his father had given up the opportunities of promotion to stay at home with his two sons) and some time before his father remarried, Paul bought him the house in Heswall, Cheshire, which is still his home today. But he was much more cautious in deciding where to live himself.

11

John Lennon, George Harrison and Ringo Starr had all bought homes in the Surrey stockbroker belt before McCartney finally made up his mind—and then he made the most character-indicative choice of all; he bought a superb house in St. John's Wood, London, close to the recording studios that he was used to using, close to his friends, and the offices of his business associates. And the result? John, George and Ringo all found themselves unhappy where they were; they all moved home in time, and yet Paul's London home is still that same London house ten years after he bought it—and now thought to be worth at least £200,000, some five times more than he paid for it before setting in hand his modernisation.

Likewise, he waited some years before deciding where to have his country home although it had been an ambition since childhood to live in Scotland; then eventually he bought a remote farm near Campbeltown (and then later another adjoining farm so that today he has an estate of nearly 600 acres). It was a choice that gave him almost total seclusion; he could seemingly vanish from the face of the earth—and twice during the Sixties when he was spending long periods pottering about the farm rumours swept the world that he was dead, and he was so remote that the rumours spread fast before the press could check the story out. At least, he *seemed* remote—just look at a small-detail map of Scotland and you will see that close to McCartney's farm is the tiny airport of Machrihanish. From there he can travel by privately hired jet—and be in London in about an hour! Which is precisely what he does.

This quality of being cautious and then making a decision that he sticks to shines through in so many other areas of his life. Take his romance with Jane Asher. For five years they were expected to marry, and made no secret of this. Eventually, on Christmas Day, 1967, they became engaged and told members of their families that they would be marrying soon. By then John Lennon, George Harrison and Ringo Starr had all married. But Paul's caution continued. Rumour had it that Jane Asher was intent on making a career for herself as an actress, and did not want to be known just as Paul McCartney's girlfriend. Whether or not that was the thing that was bothering McCartney, no-one knew but he broke off the engagement and within a few months he was living with Linda Eastman, and in March, 1969, they married. Now, unlike the Lennons, the Harrisons and the Starrs, the McCartneys' marriage has worked.

One could draw the same parallel in his attitude towards the business side of his career. In their earlier days, it was George Harrison who was the most business-minded of The Beatles—but after the death of Brian Epstein it was McCartney who tried to get The Beatles back on the road again. He produced their film "Magical Mystery Tour", and promotional clips to promote their records. He threw all his energies into making Apple a success, and by the autumn of 1968 had very nearly persuaded them to make a stage come-back (at one point the Royal Albert Hall was to be the venue for this—and then later they were planning to make a stage appearance at the Roundhouse in Chalk Farm, London, which was to have been filmed). But the others appeared to resent the fact that he was appearing to be the decision-maker, and particularly so when he suggested that Linda's father and brother-in-law (who were internationally known show business lawyers) should help to administer Apple. When the other three insisted on bringing in Allen Klein to manage Apple's affairs, it was the cautious McCartney who held back, although he co-operated with Klein and John Lennon in the battles for control of Northern Songs, he tried to persuade the others against Klein, and nearly two years passed between the date of Klein's appointment and McCartney's decision to apply to the High Court for a Receiver to be appointed. Although he was opposed by Lennon, Harrison and Starr, McCartney won the case and the Receiver was appointed.

On the extraordinary features of the relationship McCartney still has with the other Beatles is that despite the Court case and the bitter disputes that accompanied it; the public announcement that he had left the group (whereas in fact Lennon had left months earlier), and despite the bitterness that for a while spilled over into interviews and even into Lennon's work as a songwriter, it did

13

not end their friendship. Eventually, John Lennon, George Harrison and Ringo Starr all broke with Klein and started their own proceedings against him. Gradually, their breach with McCartney mended—and all four of them now help each other on different projects, meeting socially amidst widespread speculation that they will eventually record together again. The McCartneys have been guests at Lennon's home in New York and Lennon admitted then that McCartney had been right all along.

This illustrates his extraordinary strength of character. Few people would be able to repair a friendship after a dispute as deep as that, and it's a side of his personality that his public never sees. He is a one-man combination of toughness, driving ambition, artistic talent, musical skill, feel for melody, accompanied by caution, financial cunning, a perception of human nature, a memory for detail (in conversation he will discuss incidents that happened ten years earlier with total recall), a deep and abiding love for his family, a political awareness, and the natural charm of a diplomat. If there is a deeper and more calculating side to his personality, he never lets it show—though it must be said that he has a reputation within the music business for being a very tough operator, knowing exactly what he wants, and going all out to get it.

Alvin Stardust recently told me a story that demonstrates McCartney's combination of toughness and charm. Back in 1963, Stardust was known as Shane Fenton, toured with his own group The Fentones, and had had several hit singles before The Beatles even had their first. His home town was Mansfield, where his mother ran a theatrical boarding house, and when The Beatles appeared there, he called backstage to see them—and found them trapped in their dressing room, unable to go out to eat because of the vast crowd of fans waiting outside. So Stardust drove back home, and his mother packed a picnic hamper with cannisters of hot soup and a pile of salmon sandwiches. For some years after that, Stardust worked in management, and then lived overseas before starting again in Northern cabaret, and ten years went by without seeing any of The Beatles again. And then quite recently he was appearing on the BBC TV programme "Top Of The Pops"—and so was Paul McCartney with Wings. And the first thing McCartney said was: "Is your mother bringing the soup and sandwiches tonight?"

Something quite similar happened after my wife and I had had a long private interview with Paul and Linda McCartney, in which—after the interview was over—we started talking about their farmhouse in Scotland and our cottage in Devon, which is 17th century and was at one time a cider house. My wife mentioned that she was looking for some Tiffany-style lampshades, and Linda had recently found some. About a year later we attended a Wings concert at Oxford, when there was a conference for jounalists from all over the world afterwards—and McCartney suddenly called across to me: "Have you been down to Devon recently?" A few minutes later Linda asked: "Did your wife get those lampshades?"

Now, it is easy to be cynical about people who have this memory for detail—but with the McCartneys it is a very natural warmth that makes people feel they know them when in fact they probably have only a very superficial relationship. Certainly, it was this very quality that distinguished McCartney within The Beatles. I remember seeing them all at one conference when John, George and even Ringo became quite short-tempered with some of the questions that were being fired at them by different journalists—and McCartney quickly rescued the situation by giving the press just the answer they wanted with a ready smile as he did so. To have done that may have stuck in his craw for all I know but the fact that he did it undoubtedly saved the day, and prevented The Beatles receiving disastrous coverage in the next day's papers.

Yet for all this there is a widespread feeling which occasionally shows itself in conversation between musicians that McCartney is over-shadowed by Lennon, and there are even people who compare his talents adversely with those of George Harrison. One can see why people might made a judgment of this kind, for McCartney often tends to understate himself whereas Lennon is a towering figure for reasons not altogether connected with his music.

15

If the rock generation has had the impact on world thinking that I personally believe it has, and if the world's politicians now realise that the day has passed when old men could create wars for young men to die in, then the one person more than any other who has delivered that message, more effectively even than Bob Dylan, is John Lennon, with his shrewd use of images and acorns, Bagism and the Plastic Ono Band. But Lennon has only been able to do that as one-quarter of The Beatles, and as one-half of the Lennon-McCartney song-writing team he found himself with a ready made platform. And had it not been for the simplicity and melodic content of McCartney's own music, which made The Beatles' music acceptable to such a far wider audience, would Lennon ever have had such a platform?

What is so extraordinary is that the two of them—originally so raw, rough, determined, often agressive but very different people—should have found something bigger than themselves through skiffle; should have progressed from that to early Tamla Motown and rhythm 'n' blues; should have played at one stage or another practically every form of music that has been popular in the last fifty years (it is not generally realised that their stage act at the Cavern used to range from "Red Sails In The Sunset" to occasional bursts of traditional jazz and even rhythm 'n' blues oldies like "Baby Please Don't Go", with some very un-Beatle by-ways in between), and at one period they even accompanied a stripper in a strip club in Liverpool's Chinatown district, and yet out of all this developed a musical style that was new, that was fresh and quite unlike that of any of their contemporaries. Their versatility has always been quite extraordinary—and largely unknown because it is a side of their music that has seldom been seen.

I can remember once being down at a TV studio—I can't remember now whether it was the Rediffusion studios when they were appearing on "Ready, Steady Go!" or down at the BBC for "Top Of The Pops"—but they were in the studio, waiting to run through their current single so that the cameramen could check angles, and the lighting technicians could do their work. For some reason, there was a hold-up and they were kept waiting—so The Beatles stayed there on stage and ran through all the numbers in the then current pop charts, sounding first like The Kinks, then like The Rolling Stones, then The Hollies. (After all this time, I can't remember which songs they played—but it was in the days when The Beatles still wore suits, collars and ties to appear on TV.) Without them realising it, work stopped in the studio—and when they finished the technicians applauded because they were word-perfect, sound-perfect, with each number sounding just like the rival group of the day. And then whatever had gone wrong was put right—and they became The Beatles again.

This was proof of a highly developed musical skill—and one that is all the more extraordinary when you realise that these other groups sounded nothing like them. Lennon, Harrison and McCartney had developed their own style in the Liverpool ballrooms and Hamburg clubs, they were sweating in their leather suits, swearing, fighting, steaming round the halls in the back of an old van, arguing ideas, sometimes not getting paid by promoters when the popular music of the day was Frank Ifield, The Tornadoes, The Shadows, Cliff Richard, Ronnie Carroll, Alma Cogan and their like.

And to have kept going so long—McCartney and Lennon had been playing together for no less than six years before they first met Brian Epstein, and seven and a half years before their first major success—was also quite extraordinary; to have had that much experience was in itself new in the pop music of the early Sixties, and this, of course, was why they were so technically good before the success started to snowball, and why they could cope with all the pressures when they came.

In this book I will not be chronicling this success chapter by chapter. Instead, you will find all this detailed in the appendix, showing just how hard they worked day by day—though it is easy to forget now that their live stage career lasted only for a little over three and a half years after the success of "Please Please Me"—how the emphasis of their career changed, and how McCartney was the first to return to stage work.

As The Beatles, they had a reputation for being among the most reliable and punctual of all groups when it came to arriving for rehearsals, time-checks, lighting-checks, photo sessions, recording sessions or concerts—though they very quickly became almost inaccessible to people outside their own business. All this, of course, was pure professionalism. Of them all, Paul McCartney was and is the truest pro—seldom giving away a trick in an interview, bending press conferences, never letting the world outside know when something was going wrong, always smiling for the camera-men, and quick to help a fan given rough treatment by a stage-door keeper. It was the essence of good public relations—and the fans warmed to him. Beneath it all, he is every bit as tough, determined, and as aggressive as Lennon, with that rare blend of qualities that I have already mentioned. Perhaps the most remarkable thing of all is that despite all his success, and the fact that he is self-assured, dresses expensively, enjoys a high level of living and the freedom to travel anywhere in the world whenever he wants to, McCartney still has no phoney graces. His family life is totally normal. He has regular holidays amongst his wife's family in the States and his own aunts, uncles and cousins in Liverpool—and he still works at a tough pace that other people find very difficult to keep up with. I asked him why he worked himself so hard when there is clearly no financial necessity to do so, and he said: "I'm just a grafter." And I think that is probably the best word anyone could choose to describe him.

Chapter Two

It has often been suggested that all four Beatles came from a working class background of almost total anonymity, which like all rock music legends is not completely true. Certainly by the time the four of them came together their homes were in the Liverpool back streets and council estates—but John Lennon's grandfather had been a member of the Kentucky Minstrels and there was another musician in his mother's side of the family; Paul McCartney's father had been a semi-professional pianist, running his own band, Jim Mac's Jazz Band, and touring the Liverpool dance halls in the Thirties.

There were no Prime Ministers, Lord Chancellors, Judges or great literary figures or landowners tucked away in their family trees. Many of the men in Lennon's family had been clerks, and his father had been a merchant seaman. In George Harrison's family there had been a lamplighter, an engine driver and a stonemason. While the Starkeys (Ringo Starr's real name) had been living in the towns and villages around Liverpool for at least seven hundred years, though as far back as Ringo knew they had been sailors and boilermakers.

Paul McCartney's family tree is a little more complicated, suggesting that at different times the family fortunes may have wavered. As well as running that jazz band, his father—a distinguished and impressively-faced man—had worked as a cotton salesman, and going back generations before there had been fishmongers, a tobacco cutter, boilermakers and plumbers. Paul's great-great-grandfather

19

had been a Coroner, a fairly important position in Victorian England for he would be the man responsible for investigating all deaths to see that the causes were quite straight-forward, with the power to arraign a suspect on a murder charge if he thought it necessary.

In the early Sixties, The Beatles commissioned the Society of Genealogists in London to trace back their family trees—and they soon traced the McCartneys back to 1663 when Paul's ancestors were living in the Isle of Man.

But by the time Paul himself was born on 18th June, 1942, the family had been living in Liverpool for as long as any aunts, uncles or grandparents could recall. Paul himself was the first child of James and Mary McCartney. His mother was the local district nurse, and partly because of her work and also because the McCartneys kept trying to find somewhere better to live the family moved home five times by the time Paul was into his teens. His brother Michael—now also a professional musician, known as Mike McGear and best-known for his work with Scaffold—was born eighteen months later.

From all accounts, and from what Paul, Mike and their father have said to me at different times, it was a happy, very normal, largely undisturbed background—except for all those moves. Mr. McCartney was a very quiet, dignified father, who could be strict when he thought he had to be and would give both boys a hiding if that seemed to him to be what they needed. Paul and Mike were both encouraged to be polite and well-mannered—and Mrs. McCartney laid great importance on personal appearance, making sure that her sons' clothes were clean and well-pressed, that they were well-washed with their hair short and in place.

Their everyday life was little different to that of any children growing up as they were on the fringes of a large city, with green fields and streams not very far away. Like all small boys they sometimes got into mischief—like the time they stoned a bees' hives and were both badly stung, the time Paul fell into a pond and nearly drowned (Mike held on to his arm and a neighbour rescued them), and the occasion they were both caught scrumping in a nearby orchard and locked up by the farmer in his shed while he fetched their father.

To this day, the McCartney brothers are exceptionally close both to each other and to their father; there is family affection carried to a rare degree, something that stems right back to their childhood, to the example set by their mother who was loving and attentive and their father who had that blend of love, authority, humour and kindness that is the hallmark of a good parent. He would come back from work in the evenings with presents for the boys hidden behind his back, encouraged them to take an interest in the countryside, spurred Paul on when he wanted to learn guitar, bought them two rabbits when they became anxious to have a pet, bought them both new bikes, encouraged them to be active Boy Scouts and to go on camps with the local troop (sitting round a campfire in darkness was one of the first times Paul ever played guitar to an audience outside his family). Most important of all, he always made them believe—whether it was Paul appearing as a monk in a school production of Shaw's "Saint Joan" or Mike learning to play drums, or Paul thinking he might become a teacher or painter and Mike planning to be a hairdresser—that what they wanted to do really was important.

Their mother died suddenly on 31st October, 1956, after only being in hospital for two days; they were then living at 20 Forthlin Road, Liverpool 18, but the aunts and uncles rallied round, looked after the two boys until after the funeral, and for months afterwards tried to help them through this period, though it was obvious to all the family that Paul and Mike were feeling the loss keenly. It was in this family crisis that Mr. McCartney proved to be a very rare man indeed. Although on the threshold of a successful business career, he devoted all his time to his sons, staying home in the evenings to be with them, guiding them through their teens. It is not really so very surprising that the first thing Paul did when The Beatles became successful was to see that his father became secure for the rest of his days, buying a fine house in the village of Heswall, not far from Liverpool. Later, his father married again—and Paul and Mike have a close relationship with their stepmother, Mrs. Angela McCartney, and her daughter, Ruth. Every Christmas without fail Paul and Linda and the whole McCartney tribe with wives and children, aunts and uncles, cousins, nephews, and nieces gather in either Heswall or Liverpool for a family party. Likewise, the brothers are frequently together; each was Best Man at the other's wedding, and Paul has recently been working with Mike on the "McGear" album, producing it and also playing on the album with other members of Wings.

"It's only now that we realise how much our father did for us," Mike once told me in a conversation that ranged over Scaffold's work, his relationship with Paul, their home and childhood, their sentimentality, and the children's stories that have been another part of Mike's professional work.

When I asked him what he thought had made him such an emotional person, he replied: "My Mum. She died when we were still at school, and I still feel quite emotional about that. I think about her because she was great and I was very close to her. She had no idea what we were going to do when we left school because we were both so young when she died, and we never even discussed pop music with her because we weren't even thinking of that as a career ourselves. It's sad to think she's seen none of it. It would have been great if she could have seen us now. She was a good woman, and that's why I feel so sentimental about her. She was lovely. We both feel very sentimental about our childhood . . . really, I've always thought that I'm a bit like Peter Pan. At that age, you have no idea how tough you are going to have to be when you go out into the world. The knocks come later.

"The knocks have to come. They're what make you. Being knocked is good for you. It helps you to understand the world about you. My Mum's death was my first big knock.

"But my Dad taught me a lot of things; we both owe him a lot. He's a very good man, and he's a very stubborn man. He looks more like Paul than me, but I've got him

22

inside me. Of course, it would have been easy for him to have gone off with other birds when Mum died, or to have gone out getting drunk every night. But he didn't. He stayed at home and looked after us.

"He's a brilliant salesman with a very fine business brain and he could have gone right to the top in business if he had played the rules like they are now, if he had wanted to kill. He knew that to be a good businessman you have to have that killer streak, and he just wasn't prepared to be like that. And it would have meant neglecting us, and he wasn't prepared to do that, either. He told us that you have to be prepared to kill if you are to get to the top, and if he'd been prepared to pay that price he could have got there. But he was not prepared to do that—and that is the big lesson he taught us. It has rubbed off on to both of us; neither of us has really got the killer streak.

"We didn't realise it so much at the time but now Paul and I are very grateful to him, and we realise what a fine man he is. We look back now, and we think of Mum, and we see how beautiful it all was—and we understand now what he must have gone through when she died. If he had gone off with other women, and gone out getting drunk, we would have been so screwed up inside."

While Mrs. McCartney was still alive, Paul and Mike had both passed their 11-plus examinations and Paul had gone on to study at the Liverpool Institute High School, where he became a relatively skilled linguist, a keen painter and cartoonist, developing those literary interests that he has to this day. His five passes in the General Certificate of Education Ordinary-level examinations included Spanish, German and French, which encouraged his teachers and his father to think that Paul could pursue an academic career, which he started to do—planning to become a teacher—staying on at school another two years and passing the GCE Advanced level examinations in English Literature.

But long before he reached those examinations, another major influence came into Paul's life—perhaps the most crucial of all outside his family—and that was John Lennon, an altogether tougher creature, highly intelligent but

23

prepared to use his fists if he had to, already cynical by nature (though with a very tender and emotional side to him). At the same time as Paul had been studying at Liverpool Institute High School, learning guitar in the bathroom at home on an £18 instrument that his father had bought him, young Lennon was at another grammar school in the city, Quarrybank, in his fifth form, and beginning his first group, The Quarrymen.

Paul's own school was very conscious of the rock 'n' roll music that was coming across to Britain from the States with the records of Elvis Presley, Carl Perkins, Little Richard, Bo Diddley, Chuck Berry, Ray Charles, etc., and in the year below him George Harrison was already forming his first group. Also at the school at the same time were Les Chadwick, later to record as a member of Gerry and the Pacemakers, and Stu James, later a member of one of the many good early Sixties groups that failed to survive, The Mojos. Another schoolmate was the actor Bill Wainright, who has said: "I first knew Paul McCartney when we travelled on the same bus to school. He always used to wear a big overcoat with a huge fur collar. We were both keen on acting and on one occasion were both in crowd scenes in a school production of "Saint Joan". He's a born actor—and a good one . . ."

Whereas Paul's friends at the Institute were fairly conventional, perhaps going so far as to grow their hair a little longer than their parents wished (the McCartney brothers had constant battles with their father over the length of their hair) but not being really rebellious, Lennon was already kicking against the pricks. He had grown his hair long, grown his sideboards, wore drainpipe trousers and looked very Teddy Boy-ish. He was already reading the American Beat poets, devouring Kerouac—and lapping up rock 'n' roll. When they first met at the Woolton parish church fete—when Paul asked if he could play with The Quarrymen, and joined them on stage—Lennon was already a tough nut for his age.

But he soon became tougher. While Paul carried on with his school studies, Lennon left Quarrybank Grammar School and moved on to the Liverpool College of Art, thinking he might become a commercial artist or maybe a journalist. And then—in 1958—Lennon's own mother died, killed in a car accident. A mother's death in childhood or teens always leaves an impact, but in Lennon's case the effect was brutal, almost shattering; she had brought him up alone—and the accident happened just outside their home. It was witnessed by one of his childhood friends Nigel Whalley, whom he had known since the age of four, and who once told me: "It was one of those terrible things that you carry around mentally for as long as you live. I can remember the moment so well. John and I were going out together, and I called round for him just as his mother was going out shopping. We said a few words to each other. Then she crossed the street to catch a bus. I was just about to knock on the door for John when I heard the scream of brakes. I turned in a flash. I saw someone flying in the air and then fall. I ran across the verge. It was John's mother. She was just lying in the road. She didn't move. She had been hit by a car, driven by an off-duty policeman. She died in the ambulance on the way to hospital. It choked me to think I was the last person ever to speak to her."

By this time, John Lennon and Paul McCartney were already friends, visiting each other's homes to practise their guitars, still occasionally playing with The Quarrymen, whose membership frequently changed, and which eventually folded up altogether like skiffle groups all over the country. Their friendship continued—and it lasted throughout the period following the death of Mrs. Lennon, when John became increasingly rebellious, anti-authority, sometimes having disputes with his Aunt Mimi, and eventually leaving her home and moving into a flat in Gambia Terrace, Liverpool.

"The tragedy had had a terrible effect on John," remembered Nigel Whalley. "He felt so lonely after this, with no father to fall back on. He was always very bitter . . . and his humour became very weird . . . one evening, John invited us to his mother's old house in Allerton. A number of us went. We all sat round a table. John said we were going to hold a seance, and switched the lights down low. He spread letter cards round the circular table and began to rotate his hand round the top of a tumbler. The tumbler started to move and spell out words. The rest of us sat terrified. But John seemed almost unmoved. To this day, I don't know whether there was a spirit there that night or if John was just having us on . . . and he became very cutting when talking to people, often wounding with a phrase—and he didn't care who they were. One day we were picked up by the police. There were six of us, playing golf on the links at Allerton, without permission, when a squad of police came bearing down on us. We were lined up against a wall and searched. But John was not in the least worried. 'Better watch it—my dad's a copper!' he said."

This, then, was the new influence that came into Paul's life; but it was not a wholly rebellious influence—John was keen to be successful at art college, and even while he was still at Quarrybank Grammar School he had shown promise of that quite remarkable talent that later revealed itself in his two books *John Lennon In His Own Write* and *A Spaniard In The Works*. He had compiled over 250 short stories, poems, articles and cartoons while still at school—many of which were lost for years until a teacher at his old school was found to have kept a confiscated Lennon notebook titled *The Daily Howl* and another volume with the same title but different contents was found in that flat he had rented in Gambia Terrace.

As a formative influence on Paul McCartney, the importance of this period and of Lennon himself cannot be over-emphasised—for Lennon was already becoming quite a celebrity amongst Liverpool's teenage underground. Back in the early Sixties I made several long trips to Liverpool interviewing many of the people who had known him and Paul in their early days, buying up early photographs (some of which have still not been published) and back copies of the Liverpool pop paper *Mersey Beat* in which much of John Lennon's earliest work—spoofs on current songs, short stories, cartoons, etc.—first appeared under the pen-name Beatcomber.

It was one of his former flat-mates Rod Murray, who

found that missing notebook and returned it to John, who had even been back to the flat himself to try to trace it. A fan discovered two of his other missing poems "The Land of the Lunapots" and "Tales of Hermit Fred" at his old school, and then another schoolfriend Bill Turner told *Mersey Beat* that he remembered a book John produced called *The Daily Howl*. It was an exercise book filled with his stories, poems, drawings and cartoons. He used to show his work to a bloke called Pete Shotton before he let anyone else see it. Pete was his best mate at Quarrybank and I think John wrote *The Daily Howl* mainly for him. I remember it was at the time Davy Crockett was the rage and one of the poems was 'The Story of Davy Crutch-Head' . . . there were quick flashes in the book such as a weather report: 'Tomorrow will be Muggy, followed by Tuggy, Wuggy and Thuggy.' He had an obsession with Wigan Pier; forever Wigan Pier kept cropping up—mainly in a story called 'A Carrot In A Potato Mine'—and the mine was at the end of Wigan Pier. . . ."

Pete Shotton remains a close friend of Lennon and McCartney to this day. When they formed Apple, Shotton was brought in to run their shop in Baker Street—and he also ran a supermarket in Hayling Island with John as his financial backer and sleeping partner. Indeed, both Lennon and McCartney retain contact with nearly all their friends from the early days of The Quarrymen, some of whom they brought down to London to help them run Apple.

To Paul, the keen artist always coming top of his art class at school, the keen writer who won a prize presented to him by the Lord Mayor of Liverpool, this must have been a challenging milieu. For Lennon, with his taste for off-beat writers and poets, with a flat of his own and thus no need to conform, and with his genuine artistic and musical talent was a natural leader and a natural rebel. He was also a man of deep friendships and personal loyalty—I have already mentioned how Pete Shotton is a friend to this day; so, too, is Ivan Vaughan who used to be billed as "The Ace on the bass" when he played with The Quarrymen. Perhaps the deepest friendship of all, however, was

John's relationship with Stu Sutcliffe, who later joined Paul and George Harrison as a founder member of The Beatles—and is believed by some to have been the most talented of them all.

Sutcliffe was also a Liverpool art student, so talented that much of his work has been exhibited at the Walker Art Gallery in Liverpool. When The Beatles went to Hamburg in 1960, Sutcliffe fell in love with a German girl, Astrid, stayed on in Hamburg when they returned to Liverpool—and was awarded a scholarship to study art at the Hamburg University because the authorities were so impressed by his work. "Stuart was so sensitive," Astrid recalled later in an interview with the now-defunct magazine *Rave*. "He liked beautiful things. When we used to go out—which wasn't very often because I wasn't making much money and he only had his grant to college—we went to the ballet or classical concerts. He used to write stories and poems . . . he was very intelligent, very sensitive, with a wonderful sense of humour . . . he used to spend hours writing letters to John in Liverpool. He'd put down all his feelings, all his experiences, even put in illustrations and pages of poetry. These letters used to run to twenty pages or so. And John's were just as long and deep."

Then Sutcliffe—whom John and Paul had been hoping to persuade to rejoin The Beatles, making them a five-piece group again—died, not long after they had signed with Brian Epstein, and the day before they arrived in Hamburg for their fourth series of club appearances in the city. Astrid phoned Sutcliffe's mother, who flew over to Hamburg with George Harrison on the same plane; he had missed the earlier flight through feeling unwell. John and Paul arrived at the airport to meet him off the plane, and saw Astrid in tears. "Where's Stu?" they asked, and when she explained what had happened, Lennon wept almost hysterically while the other Beatles were also in tears.

This tragedy affected Lennon deeply; he collected together all Stu Sutcliffe's letters and has two of his paintings which he treasures to this day. Astrid remains a close personal friend and so, too, is her first boyfriend Klaus Voorman also an artist, whom they also met out in Hamburg. He later played with Paddy, Klaus and Gibson and then later the Manfred Mann group, later designing The Beatles' award-winning "Revolver" sleeve, and producing much of their other mid-Sixties art work. Now one of their closest musical associates, Voorman plays bass on studio sessions when they are working on different solo projects.

All this is important to remember in trying to understand the private world that surrounds McCartney and the other Beatles, because most of the really close relationships that survive today were established back in the early Sixties either in Liverpool or Hamburg. McCartney's own friendship with Lennon survived the collapse of The Quarrymen, and by then the younger George Harrison was also frequently rehearsing with them. In the years that followed, while Paul was still at school and then at work, John at college, and then George also leaving school to begin his first job, they kept meeting to write together, occasionally working as a group with different friends on drums. At one period they called themselves The Rainbows because they all had different coloured shirts; at another John and Paul worked alone as The Nurk Twins (a name that Paul and Mike McCartney had also used years earlier when entertaining at family parties); they entered a Carroll Levis talent show as Johnny and the Moondogs—and then became The Silver Beatles. All this happened while Paul was still at school. In those days, it was as much friendship as work; when not playing they still hung around together—Paul and John once went to Paris on holiday, and another time John and George went on a hitch-hiking holiday round the West Country, sleeping out on a beach one night and on a football pitch on another.

One of the things that kept them together over that five year period was that they frequently played at the Casbah, a coffee bar club in the Heyman's Green district of Liverpool, run by Mrs. Mona Best, whose son Pete was later to become their drummer. When they first played there the line-up was John Lennon, Paul McCartney, George Harrison . . . and Ken Brown.

For years, Brown was a missing part of The Beatles

Story, until I tracked him down to the outskirts of Epping Forest, where he was living in a caravan with his Jamaican-born wife, working as a shop assistant in a North London shop, but in 1958 he was in at the very start of the line-up which—with just one variation—was to become known as The Beatles.

"At that time," Brown told me, "George Harrison and I were playing with the Les Stewart Quartet. The most we ever got was two pounds for playing at a wedding reception. Working men's clubs never paid us more than ten bob (50p by today's money). It was George's girlfriend Ruth Morrison who told us that Mrs. Best was opening this coffee bar. I went round to see Mrs. Best and for the next five months we helped her get the coffee bar ready—installing lighting, covering the walls with hardboard to prevent condensation, painting the place orange and black. In return, Mrs. Best promised that we could play in the Casbah when it finally opened.

"On the Saturday it opened I went round to see Les Stewart. George was there, too, practising his guitar. Les and I got into an argument and Les said he wouldn't appear at the club. So George and I walked out. I asked George if he knew anyone who could help us out, and he said he had two mates and went off on a bus to fetch them—coming back two hours later with John Lennon and Paul McCartney. Paul was still at school with a schoolboyish haircut, and seemed rather neat, but even then John was a bit of a beatnik, wearing his hair very long over his collar, and an old pair of jeans. Among the songs we sang that night was 'Long Tall Sally,' which is one of Paul's favourite songs even today . . . and another one was 'Three Cool Cats', which John sang, rolling his eyes. This made one chap start to laugh, and John just stopped playing and said, 'Belt oop, lad!'

"John never took any nonsense from anyone even in those days. He was a lonely youngster who didn't talk much about his family . . . he seemed in need of affection, and seemed to depend on Cynthia, the girl he later married who was his steady girlfriend even when I was with them. She used to come along to the Casbah in the evenings and sit by the stage. Paul didn't bother about girls at all in those days . . ."

For nine months, the group used Brown's ten-watt amplifier as their PA system—and then came the split. One night he was not feeling too well, and Mrs. Best suggested that instead of playing with the group he should take the money on the door. Afterwards Paul McCartney objected to Brown being paid 15s (75p), the same as the rest of them, arguing that the money should be shared between John, George and himself as Brown had not been playing with them that evening.

"When Mrs. Best insisted on giving me my 15s, Paul shouted, 'Right—that's it, then', and the three of them stormed off," says Brown.

That was almost the last Ken Brown saw of John, Paul and George . . . until November, 1962, one month after the release of their first Parlophone single "Love Me Do". One day that November he received a telephone call from Neil Aspinall, who was now The Beatles road manager and had given up what seemed a promising career as a trainee accountant after their first visit to Hamburg to become their full time (and very underpaid) driver.

"He said the boys were in a bit of a jam," Ken Brown remembered. "They had blown all their money and Brian Epstein wouldn't let them have any more . . . now they had to go up to Sheffield for a gig, and he said they would have to sleep rough in the back of the van if they couldn't raise some more money. Neil asked me to lend them £20 and I agreed. They all turned to collect it, but only Neil came to the door. The others didn't even get out of the van. Marcia, my wife, and I went to exchange a few words with them, and I handed over the money. 'We'll drop in and see you one night,' said Paul, as they drove off."

Spending all their money was an endemic Beatle disease. Larry Parnes has recalled in a radio interview that after he booked The Beatles in October, 1960, for a two-week ballroom tour of Scotland backing singer Johnny Gentle, he received an agonised call from John Lennon at his London office, asking: "Where's the bloody money?"—on the opening day of the tour!

Paul McCartney was then still at school and expected by his father and his headmaster to go on to teacher training college; but the chance of a tour—even for only £15 a week—was too much to resist. And off he went. Then after that he went off to Hamburg—receiving a message from his headmaster asking him to visit the head's office. So he wrote from Hamburg, saying he had resigned from the school. Later he told the magazine *Rave*: "I said, 'Dear sir, I've got a great job in Germany and I'm earning fifteen pounds.'"

Johnny Gentle told me that when he first saw The Beatles it was quite a shock. "I wondered what on earth Parnes had sent me. They were about the roughest looking bunch I had seen in my life, hopelessly fitted out with no stage gear. Paul and Stu had black shirts. I lent John a shirt of mine and we went out and bought one for George—but we were so broke that we couldn't afford to buy one for the drummer, so he wore white. The promoter, Duncan McKinnon, thought they were no good and wanted to sack them at the end of the first week. So, we all sat down together in a bar in Inverness and went over each number until the boys had got the sound right. They were terribly depressed, and I felt sorry for them—and persuaded McKinnon to let them finish the second week. One night, after we'd finished a show, a girl came up and asked for their autographs. John was so thrilled; he couldn't stop talking about it—and even asked me if I thought they should chuck up everything and go full time. He was still talking about it when our Dormobile crashed into another car at the crossroads in Banff. The boys were thrown all over the place and the van was almost a write-off.

"We said goodbye to each other at Dundee railway station, and as my train pulled out, they were still saying, 'Ask Larry Parnes if he wants us again!'"

Another of their stranger bookings was as the backing group to a stripper called Janice, who appeared in a night club in Liverpool's Chinatown district. "We all wore pink, shiny suits and played weird music," Paul McCartney recalled. "Each time she finished her act, she'd turn right round, stark naked, and look us straight in the eye. We were still only lads and didn't know where to put ourselves." In an interview with another defunct pop magazine *Hit Parade,* they recalled that Janice gave them music to play—some classical music including the "Spanish Fire Dance". But as they couldn't read music, this was of no use—and they made do with "The Harry Lime Theme"!

All in all, their pre-Hamburg and pre-Cavern experiences were distinctly off-beat—for a time they even went through a beat poetry phase, backing a then fairly well-known "beat" figure, the bearded writer Royston Ellis, who wrote the books *Jiving To Gyp, Rave, The Rainbow Walking Stick, The Big Beat Scene* and with Jet Harris, *Driftin' with Cliff Richard* as well as a biography of The Shadows. He appeared with The Beatles at another of the early Liverpool venues, the Jacaranda in Slater Street, where they were booked regularly in 1960 and 1961. Two of their former girlfriends, Pat Davis and Ann Kay, worked there as waitresses.

"It was The Beatles who first brought us to the Jacaranda," Ann told me. "They were always there in those days; it was their second home. They used to sit round drinking cups of coffee in between sessions in the basement. But in those days they had no microphones or expensive equipment. Girls used to take it in turns in the audience to hold up their mikes—just the headpieces tied to broom sticks. There were four of us who used to go round with The Beatles—Pat, Louie Steel, Linda Robinson and myself. We were crazy about all four of them, particularly Paul. He had a kind, gentle way with him, and sent us all lovely Christmas cards. He was the only one of The Beatles who could dance, and in between sessions at the different halls and clubs he would come down on the floor and join in dancing with us. He was smashing.

"Nearly every night the boys took us about in their van. To Preston one night, then Whitchurch another—and to all the places they used to play in Liverpool; Aintree Institute and so on."

The owner of the Jacaranda (which was known as "The Jack" to all the Liverpool groups of the day) was Alan Williams, who also owned The Blue Angel, a drinking club to which they would all return late at night after their gigs. At the time he was also manager to The Beatles as well as several of the other big Liverpool groups of the day like Rory Storm and the Hurricanes (who were later produced by Brian Epstein and who then had Ringo Starr as their drummer), Gerry and the Pacemakers (who later had a string of No. 1 hits with Epstein as their manager), The Big Three (also managed by Epstein, though briefly), Howie Casey and the Seniors (Casey is still a working musician, now mainly associated with John Entwistle of The Who's solo projects), and Derry Wilkie, who occasionally sang with The Beatles when they later started appearing at The Cavern. Of The Beatles, Williams subsequently told *Melody Maker*: "When they played for me in the Jacaranda it was 'til three in the morning and maybe that was for a pound a head, something like that. But everybody used to get up and have a jam session."

But all this was pre-Hamburg, and it was—as they admit themselves—Hamburg that made them. And it was Williams who made the first bookings for them to appear in Hamburg, and who still has the original contracts—for them to play four and a half hours a night Tuesdays to Fridays, and then six hours a night on Saturdays and Sundays, all for thirty marks a day each.

Although at the time, The Beatles were wildly excited about the offer of a trip to Germany—they were only the second Liverpool group to go to Germany, and Paul McCartney had considerable difficulty persuading his father that he be allowed to go—that first trip turned out to be a disaster.

They had been booked to appear at the Indra Club, which was on the Reeperbahn, an area of strip clubs and clip joints, patrolled by pimps and hookers. When the club was closed on the orders of the police, they moved on to the Kaiserkeller, where they lived in an attic—and from whence they were later deported. On the later trip they appeared at the Top Ten Club, again sharing an attic—this time with another British singer Tony Sheridan, also an ex-art school student, originally from Norwich. Then on their later visits they appeared at the newly opened Star

Club. Their five visits to Hamburg were one of the crucial stages in the making of The Beatles as a group and their individual development as musicians; it was there that they recorded for the first time, backing Tony Sheridan in sessions for Polydor—and it was there that they first had the experience of playing up to six hours a night, which proved an invaluable tightening-up process for their music, as their followers quickly noticed when they returned to Liverpool after each trip.

Before that first trip, they had been playing with a succession of different drummers, none of whom wanted to go to Germany—and once he had persuaded his father to allow him to go Paul McCartney phoned Pete Best. "Paul said, 'Do you want to come to Germany?' bellowing down the phone. I jumped at the chance, and he said, 'Right. Get your things packed—we're going tomorrow!' And that was that. I was a Beatle."

Among the people who remember them in Hamburg are Peter Eckhorn, who was then the owner of the Top Ten Club, which was where he was when they turned up one night. He later told *Record Mirror*: "They were working at 'the Kaiserkeller in Hamburg at the time, but they didn't like it there and so they came to see me and ask if there was any work to be had at the Top Ten. To show what they could do they played a couple of numbers for me. I liked them. I said okay, I'd give them a job. But before I could hire them the owners of the Kaiserkeller made a complaint about the boys to the police, saying they'd tried to set fire to the club. It wasn't true, of course, but the complaint had the desired effect. The Beatles were deported. It took seven months to get them back again . . . they stayed three months (on the second trip) and were very popular, not so much for their music (which wasn't so different from the other groups), but for their personalities . . ."

Stories about that first trip to Hamburg are very confused, but what appears to have happened—from what Pete Best and Tony Sheridan have told me, and from what The Beatles have said on the few occasions they have talked about it, is that there had been trouble at the Kaiserkeller, where The Beatles would mimic the Nazis on stage, goose-step as part of their act and yell "Sieg Heil", and there had been frequent fights in the audience. Then one night there was a fire at their flat. The fire brigade were called—and the police stepped in. They were taken down to the local police station where George was found to be under the age of eighteen, and John was found to have no work permit—and with Paul and Pete they were advised rather firmly to get back home to Liverpool. (Stu Sutcliffe stayed on in Hamburg.)

Returning to England, they very nearly broke up—and Paul McCartney's father was quite adamant that the time had come for him to get a job. In the evening, they still met—and from all the accounts I have been told it would appear that it was only the encouragement of Mrs. Best, who had given them their start at the Casbah Club, and Neil Aspinall, who had given up his job as a trainee chartered accountant to drive them and who drew up giant posters for them billing them as "DIRECT FROM HAMBURG," that in fact encouraged them to keep going. Using an old red and white van, with a can of water by the front seat because the radiator leaked, Neil drove them to their gigs—and on 27th December, 1960, just after their return from Hamburg, The Beatles appeared at Litherlands Town Hall.

Neil, now one of the chief executives at Apple and still one of their most trusted friends, later told me: "When Paul launched into 'Long Tall Sally' the effect was sensational. Before they went to Germany, The Beatles had been just another group. But now they really had something. Girls started screaming and tried to rush the stage. None of us had seen anything like it before."

From that night, The Beatles were Liverpool's top group—earning six pounds a night. But it was to be two years before they became known outside Liverpool and Hamburg, and there was still pressure on Paul McCartney at home to get a secure, steady job.

Very few people thought they could make a career out of their music. Paul's father had very grave doubts—and Nigel Whalley's father had been among those who had advised them: "There's no future in that kind of thing. You'd best drop it—and get your hair cut as well!"

In recent years, Paul has likened what kept them going to "a sort of blind Bethlehem star," a belief that though they did not know where they were going they were at least going somewhere, and, above all, the fact that they did enjoy the music they were making—for by now Paul and John were starting to write their own material together.

Still under family pressure to get a more conventional job, Paul later told the *New Musical Express* that he "had a bit of a conscience towards me Dad. One day he TOLD me to go out and get a job, so I went down to the Labour Exchange in me donkey jacket and jeans . . . the fellow sent me to an electrical firm called Massey and Coggins—they were electrical engineers, actually. I told the boss I wanted a job. I wasn't particular, I said. I'd sweep the yard if he wanted. But he asked me where I'd been educated, and when I said Liverpool Institute he started making big plans. They gave me this job of winding coils for about seven pounds a week—big money then. At work they called me Mantovani because of the long hair. Anyway, I was hopeless. Everybody else used to wind fourteen coils a day, while I'd get through one and a half—and mine were the ones that never worked! After a bit I started getting lunch-time dates playing at the Cavern. I had to whip out of work over the back wall at lunch time and go in the next day and say I'd been ill. One day I just didn't go in and that was that . . ." And then he got another job as a lorry driver's mate, starting at 6:30 am in the morning, and often exhausted after playing late the night before.

The dream was still success as a musician, and when they were invited to go back to Hamburg, Paul again jumped at the chance, even though this time they were again living in an attic flat, sharing it with Tony Sheridan, the singer with whom they made those first records, which were subsequently released in this country by Polydor (see first appendix). They stayed there three months.

"It was a pretty grim way to live," Sheridan told me. "It was Bohemian—just this one attic with no windows . . . I shared a room with Paul and Pete, and John and George were in another with Stu, and they just used to sleep there, because they were exhausted by the time they finished playing at the club, where they were often on stage eight hours a night . . . The only light we had in that flat was a fanlight in the roof, which leaked, and when it rained we were soaked. There were no carpets and there was no heating—and no running water, just a basin and a stand, and a jug of water for washing. There were these six Army bunks strewn about the two rooms, and for months we lived on nothing but cornflakes as the place got filthier and filthier . . . we kept our bedclothes for a month or so at a time, because we couldn't afford to get them cleaned."

In a similar interview with the *New Musical Express*, Sheridan said: "We all lived in an attic . . . bare boards, freezing draughts, the lot. Bit like Oliver Twist! There were bunk beds. John used to have the top bunk and he'd crash around when he got up because he could never see a thing without his glasses. Once he started banging around we all had to get up. John was a wild character in those days. The others were a little quieter, but there wasn't much in it. They were all ravers . . . our day began at about two in the afternoon, when we would swagger down to the Seamen's Mission for a meal. I don't know why but we always used to have the same meal. All the time, everywhere. Tea and cornflakes."

It was while they were living there, meeting the other groups who were also out in Hamburg either at the Seaman's Mission or in the late night bars, that they were spotted by Bert Kaempfert. Now one of the world's most successful recording artistes himself, with his own studio orchestra that has worked with him on many of his best-selling albums; Kaempfert is also the composer of such standard songs as "Strangers In The Night" (which he wrote originally as an instrumental for the film "A Man Could Get Killed") and "Spanish Eyes" (which also started off as an instrumental); but then he was contracted to Polydor as one of their A & R (artistes and repertoire) men. It was he who saw The Beatles playing one night, and suggested they record with Sheridan. These were the sessions that produced "Cry For A Shadow," "My Bonnie," "Ain't She Sweet," "Take Out Some Insurance On Me Baby," "What'd I Say?," "The Saints," "Why" and "Nobody's Child," on some of which they played alone and on others accompanied Sheridan (see first appendix).

And it was one of those tracks that was to prove the turning point in their career, which was to lead to their world-wide success and to everything else that Paul McCartney and the other Beatles have since achieved.

Chapter Three

The track that was to prove so vital to the future careers of The Beatles was "My Bonnie." After recording it in Hamburg early in 1961, it was released as a single in Germany. Not surprisingly they had a few copies with them in Liverpool, which they would occasionally play on the house record player during intervals at The Cavern, where they were now appearing regularly, and at the other venues in the area where they were now in demand.

The Liverpool beat group movement was thriving; there were venues all round the city suburbs, that major central venue The Cavern, the coffee bars like the Jacaranda where the groups all met socially by day, The Blue Angel where they all went drinking by night, and they even had their own newspaper, *Mersey Beat*. But outside Liverpool and outside the generation that followed the groups, all this was largely unknown . . . until 28th October, 1961.

That was the day when one young teenager walked into the Nems record store in Whitechapel and asked the man behind the counter if he had a record called "My Bonnie" by The Beatles. The man standing there was Brian Epstein, whose family owned the Nems group of shops. He had never heard of The Beatles, but promised to search out a copy of the single if he could find one—and then two girls came into the shop and they, too, asked if he had this record by The Beatles. Epstein was astute enough to realise that three queries for one unknown record was significant, and when a friend told him that The Beatles appeared regularly at The Cavern, he decided to go down there and see them for himself, which he duly did on 9th November, 1961.

That in itself was remarkable for Brian Epstein was from a totally different background to The Beatles, and not at all the sort of person that you would have expected to have found in those days listening to a group at The Cavern, but because he was a director of Nems, which was the leading record store in Liverpool, he was treated as a celebrity at The Cavern, and his presence announced from the stage. Even this he found discomfiting, though he subsequently went up to the stage and introduced himself to the group—later inviting them to meet him at the Nems offices. By the time they did so, he had already sold over 100 copies of that "My Bonnie" record, which he imported from Germany to meet the local demand.

But when the day for the meeting came, Paul was not there—which did not amuse Epstein at all. "Where is he?" he asked the other three, and George Harrison explained that Paul was having a bath. "But he'll be late," said Epstein, a neat, very conventional, public school educated man. "Yes—but very clean," said Harrison.

Somewhere deep down inside Epstein, there was an artistic talent seeking to find expression; of that there is no doubt, though I must confess that the first time I met him I found him a distinctly unimpressive figure and gained the impression (which may or may not have been a true one) that when The Beatles became successful he didn't really know what had hit him. But somewhere, deep down, well below the surface of this conventionally dressed man, with his dark grey striped suits, short hair, clean shaven features and polite but very conventional conversation there must have been something. When only ten years old he had been expelled from Liverpool College not for doing anything sensational but because the school thought he was below their usual standard; then he went to a Jewish boarding school near Tunbridge Wells, and thereafter failed his entrance examinations to several major British public schools, among them Rugby and Repton, though he eventually was admitted to Wrekin College, which he left before his sixteenth birthday with no scholastic achieve-

42

ments of any kind behind him. But, as I say, deep down something stirred . . . indeed he eventually persuaded his family to allow him to become a student at the Royal Academy of Dramatic Art, after having been discharged on medical grounds from the Army after a particularly unimpressive period of National Service as a private in the Royal Army Service Corps.

At RADA, his career was equally undistinguished—though it must be said in all fairness that he was part of one of RADA'S better intakes, a contemporary of Susannah York, Tom Courtenay, Sean Phillips (wife of Peter O'Toole) and Joanna Dunham. After finishing his course at RADA, he returned home to Liverpool, seemingly destined as the family's eldest son to rise from shop assistant to director in the family business, which included furniture stores as well as that record shop.

Anyway, failure though he might have been at everything else in his life, Epstein saw something in The Beatles that touched a chord. Even though he was very annoyed when Paul McCartney failed to turn up on time for his first interview with them, and though Paul was also reluctant to sign a contract with him, Epstein persevered, offered to manage the group, and subsequently—despite his family's considerable doubts—proceeded to throw all his energies into their management.

The first thing he did was clean them up. He was subsequently to describe that first day he had seen them at The Cavern in his autobiography *A Cellarful of Noise*: they "were not very tidy and not very clean. But they were tidier and cleaner than anyone else who performed at that lunchtime session or, for that matter, at most of the sessions I later attended. I had never seen anything like The Beatles on any stage. They smoked as they played and they ate and talked and pretended to hit each other. They turned their backs on the audience and shouted at them and laughed at private jokes. But they gave a captivating and honest show and they had very considerable magnetism . . ."

Epstein persuaded them to start wearing suits, collared shirts and ties. He insisted on total professionalism, on turning up on time for every engagement or personal interview, however insignificant it might appear to be—and he played what I still believe to be a masterstroke, booking major stars of the day like Little Richard, Joe Brown, Bruce Channel, to appear with The Beatles at the major venues on Merseyside, so that his group could be seen by local audiences to be just as good. He also wrote to Bert Kaempfert at Polydor in Germany asking under what conditions he would be prepared to release them from the three-year contract they had signed with Kaempfert; but he imposed no conditions—he let them go.

Throughout late 1961 and 1962, Epstein continued to work in the family business, of which he was by then a director—with his work as The Beatles' manager running parallel. Now they were earning up to thirty pounds a night—but not every night. He was also hiring halls and promoting them himself. But he knew, just as they did, that the most important thing of all was for them to secure a contract with one of the major British recording companies. And this was easier said than done; they were turned down by Decca, by Pye and by several of the executives within EMI before another of EMI's label managers, George Martin of Parlophone, offered them a contract in May, 1962.

Their first main recording session was early in September, and the Liverpool pop paper *Mersey Beat,* which had been closely following each stage in their career, reported in issue number 31: "At 8:15 on the morning of Tuesday, September 4, believe it or not The Beatles assembled on the tarmac of Liverpool airport. The boys were in great form (even at that early hour) although they were subjected to a somewhat bumpy and tiring flight. Their manager was travelling with London promoter and agent Don Arden (on whom The Beatles impressed their personalities—of course). After registering at their Chelsea hotel they arrived at EMI's studios in St. John's Wood. Number 2 studio was prepared and their A and R manager George Martin with his assistant Ron Richards were awaiting their arrival, and so was their road manager Neil Aspinall, who had safely transported their equipment from Liverpool.

"And so the moment came that so many aspirants long for, the moment when all was set to make a first disc. A first disc with the world's greatest recording organisation. The rehearsal part of the session began. It was a long and hard afternoon's work. Six numbers were considered and eventually two were selected for the actual recording session in the evening. Between sessions George Martin took The Beatles out for dinner at his favourite Italian restaurant. During the meal, to the delight of the group, he recounted his experiences when recording Peter Sellers and Spike Milligan. And then the session proper. "Love Me Do" was no simple matter. Everyone was anxious to attain a perfect sound which would reproduce The Beatles' unique qualities exactly. The backing (the voices were superimposed later) was "taken" no less than fifteen times—John's mouth (on harmonica) was numb with playing and the atmosphere was tense. When the vocals had been recorded and the session ended (at midnight) everyone was so dazed and tired that it wasn't really known how good or bad was the result. The Beatles' manager was left in no doubt as to the result when he heard the disc in George Martin's office the next morning. His reaction, like George's was of great delight."

It was not only in the studios at EMI that there was tension; as the months passed without any sign that The Beatles were actually getting anywhere, more and more family pressure was brought on Brian Epstein to give up what was clearly thought a flight of fancy and concentrate on his work within the family business. While within The Beatles there was tension over the sacking of Pete Best and his replacement as drummer by Ringo Starr. Precisely how and why that happened will probably be a confused story for as long as people write about The Beatles—but what is clear is that there was some unhappiness about Pete Best's work as a drummer. In his autobiography *A Cellarful of Noise* Brian Epstein said "George Martin had not been too happy about Pete Best's drumming and The Beatles, both in Hamburg and at home had decided his beat was wrong for their music. I wasn't sure about that and was not anxious to change the membership of The Beatles at a time when they were developing as personalities. So I tried to talk to Pete about his drumming, without hurting his feelings and at the same time I asked The Beatles to leave the group as it was. They, however, had decided that sooner or later they wanted Pete to leave. They thought him too conventional to be a Beatle and though he was friendly with John, he was not with George and Paul. And one night in September the three of them approached me and said: 'We want Pete out and Ringo in.' "

It was Epstein who broke the bad news to Pete Best, and I must say in all fairness to Best that his own version and the versions I subsequently heard from other people close to The Beatles at the time are at slight variance with that account of Epstein's. What is also clear is that at the time Best was for many fans the most popular Beatle—and when they sacked him this led to some very unpleasant incidents at their appearances in the Liverpool clubs. Fans started chanting "Pete forever, Ringo never" when they appeared on stage; there were some scuffles; George Harrison had his eye blacked—and for two nights Epstein said he was afraid to go anywhere near The Cavern.

So there there was one undoubted cause of tension; another was that the new recruit, Ringo Starr, felt far from secure—he turned up at one recording session to find another man, a session drummer, sitting on the drum seat. Later Ringo told the *New Musical Express*: "George Martin said he wanted me to play tambourine on the session. You can imagine how I felt. He obviously thought the first record wasn't good enough because of my drumming . . ." And although he had known the other Beatles for some years, even playing with them occasionally at sessions at the Kaiserkeller in Germany and the Odd Spot in Liverpool, he was still not regarded as an intimate by John, Paul and George. They did not even tell him that John had married, with Paul McCartney as Best Man—in that same *New Musical Express* interview he said: "I found out when we went to see an accountant about our tax and John started claiming for a dependent. The other two knew. It was natural, I suppose. He wanted it kept secret at that time and I still wasn't on the inner circle."

46

All in all, it was not a happy period for The Beatles, but they kept going with that strange Bethlehem star that Paul McCartney refers to to guide them. During 1962 they received their first-ever award in a popularity poll conducted by *Mersey Beat*; made three more trips to Hamburg, appearing at the newly opened and more prestigious Star Club—their last trip was just before Christmas after "Love Me Do" had been released in Britain, creeping into the lower reaches of the music paper charts. Before they went, they recorded the follow-up single with George Martin "Please Please Me"—and left for Germany with no idea that this was the record that was to be the start of everything for them.

In Hamburg it was a hard winter, with snow deep on the streets and harsh winds blowing in from the sea. On Christmas Day they went to a party with friends—and ate fish with horse radish sauce for their Christmas Dinner. On Boxing Day, they were the guests of the owner of the Star Club, Manfred Weissleder, at a traditional roast turkey and Christmas crackers party with Liverpool friends Kingsize Taylor and the Dominoes, the American group Johnny and the Hurricanes and their old friend Tony Sheridan.

At the beginning of January they flew back to Britain, straight into a Scottish ballroom tour. "Please Please Me" was released on 11th January and the following week had entered the music paper charts. They were quickly booked on to a theatre tour with Helen Shapiro, Danny Williams and Kenny Lynch—and before the tour ended the record was at No. 1, they were stopping the show every night with their stage act and squeezing in TV dates in between. They were working to such a tight schedule that in just one day they recorded all the tracks for their first album, which also took the title "Please Please Me."

Everything happened so quickly in those early months of 1963; by the summer they had had three Number One records—"Please Please Me," "From Me To You" and "She Loves You." Their theatre tours followed each other in quick succession—first touring with Helen Shapiro, then beginning another tour with Tommy Roe and Chris Montez, and then

47

following that with another tour with Roy Orbison and Gerry and the Pacemakers. In between there were constant TV and radio appearances, interviews with the music papers and photo sessions, ballroom appearances when they were not on tour, and then in the summer weeks in variety at Margate, Weston-super-Mare, Llandudno, Southport and Bournemouth.

At first, the music business found it hard to understand this sudden arrival of what had been a totally unknown group. I was then working part-time on the *New Musical Express,* laying out their news pages every Wednesday—and can clearly remember the phone calls from famous agents handling artistes who had until then been the country's biggest pop stars and couldn't believe what was happening. On the *New Musical Express* itself, a young writer from Merseyside Alan Smith, who became very close to The Beatles and whose wife later worked for them at Apple, tried to persuade the rest of the staff that something sensational was happening on that first Helen Shapiro tour—and they did not believe him.

What in fact happened during 1963 was that the artistes who had been stars up until the beginning of that year suddenly found they could not get work; the solo performers in the main vanished—and the record company "scouts" descended on Liverpool like a pack of locusts trying to sign up any other groups working in the city rumoured to be as good as The Beatles. But Brian Epstein had got in first; that year he launched Gerry and the Pacemakers, who had three Number One hits one after the other; Billy J. Kramer and the Dakotas, who had four huge hits, two of them going to Number One; Cilla Black, who was to become one of the major artistes of the Sixties and Seventies; The Fourmost, The Big Three, The Remo Four, Tommy Quickly, Michael Haslam, The Rustiks (the latter three did not come from Liverpool). Practically every recording company in the land had at least one Liverpool group on its books—and what became known as "The Mersey Sound" or "The Liverpool Sound" swept the country, sweeping the stars of the year before into oblivion.

It was one of the most sudden phenomena the music

business had ever seen; there has been nothing like it since—neither the Mods nor the Flower Power phases had anything like this power and intensity.

In Liverpool, there were literally several hundred teenagers who thought their chance had come—bands like The Escorts, The Dennisons, Kingsize Taylor and the Dominoes, The Searchers, Faron's Flamingoes, The Coasters, The Seniors, Lee Curtis and the All Stars, Earl Preston and The Realms, The Cordes, The Kinsleys, The Swinging Blue Jeans, Gerry de Ville and the City Kings, The Mosquitos, The Kubas, Rory Storm and the Hurricanes, The Shakers, Mark Peters and the Silhouettes, The Undertakers, The Mojos, Beryl Marsden, Ian and the Zodiacs, Earl Royce and the Olympics, The Blackwells, The Merseybeats, Sonny Webb and the Cascades, Freddie Starr and the Midnighters, Cass and the Casanovas, Johnny Sandon, The Dimensions, and so the list could go on.

Some of them became successful; The Searchers had several hit records—and the Mojos, the Swinging Blue Jeans and the Merseybeats all had some success. But many of the groups perished, more often than not through lack of capital on the part of their management and the inability to keep up hire purchase payments than through lack of talent. The human tragedies of Liverpool in the early Sixties were hundredfold—so much optimism and so much failure. The only real survivors were those who Brian Epstein signed and launched right at the very beginning of it all.

The Beatles themselves—Paul McCartney and John Lennon had now known each other eight years, and George Harrison five years—seized every opportunity, and set a pace for themselves that few could keep up with. Their seasons in Hamburg had given them the strength to do that.

Perhaps the strangest feature of the whole year was that pop music (no-one used the term "rock music" in those days) became in a very real sense a popular movement; this was the people's choice, the music they wanted—and for the first time the teenagers of Britain chose their own stars. It took time for people to realise that the old days of balding agents puffing cigars as they signed contracts on tables swilling with champagne had gone. At first, the old-established agents tried to foist new groups on the teenagers as rivals to The Beatles, but the fans wouldn't have it. Likewise the record companies tried to find the next big sound—but the audience wouldn't have that, either. The old-established techniques for launching new artistes went by the board; it was no longer enough to choose a singer with a pretty face, pay a group of musicians a weekly wage to accompany him on stage, book him into the right TV shows—and call him a star. All that no longer worked; to survive in the new era you had to be good, you had to be tough and you had to have talent—and that as much as their music was the big contribution that came from The Beatles.

Looking back, one of the strangest features of the year was that until the autumn the national press had no idea what was happening in the country; the old stars who could not get work were still featured in the national press while the new groups who were selling records by the hundred thousand received barely a mention. I remember late in the summer of 1963 trying to persuade the daily papers to take a story I had written on Paul McCartney's romance with Jane Asher, which I knew would be of major interest to the country's teenagers; no paper was interested—even though this was an exclusive story—for the very simple reason that they did not know who Paul McCartney was. I tried every national paper, and when I explained Paul was one of The Beatles, the response was either laughter or "Who are The Beatles?" And by then they had had three Number One hit records! (Even funnier, in retrospect, is the fact that when I later had another exclusive story that their song publishing company Northern Songs Ltd. was to be floated on the Stock Exchange, no paper in Fleet Street would believe me—and one City Editor told me he thought I was crackers to believe that The Beatles' songs could generate that much income!)

But all that changed in the autumn of 1963. On 13th October The Beatles topped the bill for the first time on what was then the country's top television show "Sunday

Night At The London Palladium"—and their fans blocked all the streets around the theatre, causing chaos throughout the day while they were rehearsing, and screaming so loud that their voices could be heard inside the theatre. Police had to be called to control the crowds, and faced with a demonstration of public opinion of that order even Fleet Street had to sit up and take notice. Which they did; soon it was difficult to find a newspaper that was not running serials, a photo-feature, an interview or an article—often written by people claiming an intimacy with the group which they did not possess. In many ways, the story of their success is rich in comedy of this kind; Epstein was to complain in *A Cellarful of Noise* that it took him nearly eighteen months to get the press interested in the group.

Thereafter, practically everything The Beatles did became public knowledge; their recording sessions, their rehearsals, their TV appearances, their concert tours, their triumph in the Royal Variety Show, their tailoring sessions with Duggie Millings, their trips to Sweden and Paris, their highly successful films "A Hard Day's Night" and "Help!," their triumphs in the States after their first breakthrough in February,1964, their new homes, their marriages, their children, their new cars, the success of their records (each of which went straight to Number One in the charts), their awards in the music paper polls, their M.B.E.s, their opinions on most known subjects, John Lennon's reunion with his father, the riots that followed some personal appearances, the way they looked after their families . . . it is all there in the first appendix, told in chronological order, which shows just how hard they worked, and what they accomplished between then and August, 1966, when The Beatles gave their last concert together at Candlestick Park, San Francisco.

For four years, The Beatles were constantly in the news, probably working harder than any performers before them. For most of that time Paul McCartney's constant companion was Jane Asher, whom he was widely expected to marry, though Epstein said rather pointedly in *A Cellarful of Noise* that Paul was well aware that marriage might be harmful to his career.

When The Beatles first became successful early in 1963, Paul was still living at home with his father and brother Michael in Forthlin Road, Liverpool; it had been their home since before his mother died—and being close to his family Paul kept returning there whenever there was a gap in The Beatles' schedule. Soon his home address became known, and a crowd of girls would be waiting on the doorstep from early morning until late at night, hoping for a glimpse of McCartney, who would often stay out of sight—though sometimes if the crowd was not too large he would come to the door and sign autographs.

In the early months of 1963, The Beatles stayed regularly at the same hotel—the President in Russell Square, London; but this became known so they moved on to other hotels, and then later—as they had to spend more and more time down in London—Epstein arranged for them all to stay at a rented flat in Green Street, Mayfair, another address which quickly became known to teenagers all over Britain, who were soon camping outside the door (it was quite astonishing how quickly news of a Beatle's address spread).

They only stayed together at Green Street for a very short time, more weeks than months; partly to avoid the crowds. Then John Lennon and his then wife Cynthia and their son Julian moved out to Weybridge; Ringo Starr later moved nearby, and George Harrison bought a bungalow in Esher.

But Paul just went to ground; at the time, the fans were thrown off the scent . . . they did not know it, but he was spending nearly all his time at the Ashers' home in Wimpole Street, where he had his own room, became a close friend of Jane's brother Peter—later one half of the pop duo Peter and Gordon who had a world-wide hit with the Lennon-McCartney song "World Without Love"—and virtually became a part of their family.

Chapter Four

Paul McCartney's relationship with Jane Asher lasted five years, and even before Linda Eastman came into his life he was a very different man from the leather suited rocker who had toured the Hamburg clubs. As The Beatles' career progressed through the mid-Sixties he more than John, George or Ringo seized the opportunity to widen his interests, to extend his knowledge and to broaden his whole lifestyle.

He smartened himself up, started wearing expensively tailored three-piece suits, had his shirts made specially for him to his own designs, started a fashion in high heeled leather boots, dined well—and rapidly put on weight (he had always had a tendency to be chubby in his teens, and had only lost it working in the sweaty Hamburg clubs— his father had been quite shocked by the physical change in him when Paul returned from Germany). He bought himself one of the most expensive cars on the market, a blue Aston Martin DB6, and became a regular at the most fashionable clubs of the mid-Sixties. At the old Ad Lib Club he used to have his own table reserved just inside the door on the right, and as other clubs opened he and Jane became regulars at the Scotch of St James and then later The Rasputin, The Bag O'Nails and The Revolution.

But he was more than just a successful man-about-town. Usually accompanied by Jane, he attended nearly all the London theatrical productions; under her mother's tuition he learned to play the recorder (which is a difficult instrument to master, though this is not generally realised as the recorder is used so widely in primary schools for music-making of a rather primitive form); he learned to write music in the traditional sense of using pen and paper (even today most rock songwriters cannot actually "read" music but tend to use a tape recorder to keep a note of their ideas); he returned to painting which had been one of his main interests at school in Liverpool; with the increased leisure time that The Beatles had when their days of touring and live appearances ceased, he began reading extensively the works of most leading European and American writers. On a totally amateur basis he started making films, keeping all his equipment at the home he acquired in St John's Wood, and he began building up a wide-ranging collection of classical albums ranging through the traditional composers like Brahms, Mozart and Beethoven to modern theorists like Stockhausen.

Jane Asher undoubtedly had a considerable influence upon him. She had been a well-known young actress long before The Beatles went to Hamburg or met Brian Epstein; indeed, she had already made her first film appearance long before Paul McCartney passed his 11-plus and was all set for a career in the theatre before he had even played his first note on a guitar—but she was still nearly four years younger than he was.

Born in London on 5th April, 1946, she was the daughter of Dr. Richard Asher, who became known as a writer and broadcaster, though his main work was as a consultant in blood and mental diseases at the Central Middlesex Hospital. Her mother was a professional musician, teaching oboe at the Royal Academy of Music. Jane had just the one brother, Peter. He later became a singer as one-half of the Peter and Gordon duo, toured the states several times and also toured Australia, New Zealand and throughout Europe after the world-wide success of their number one hit single "World Without Love."

Jane, who also had a younger sister, Clare, made her first appearance at the age of five in the highly praised film "Mandy," in which she played a deaf mute. At the age of twelve, she made her first stage appearance as Alice in "Alive In Wonderland" at the Oxford Playhouse, and the following summer appeared in the play "The Housemaster" at Frinton. In 1960, she received exceptional reviews from the critics for her acting in the film "The Greengage Summer" with Kenneth More and Susannah York, and at the age of fourteen she became the youngest actress ever to play the part of Wendy in the history of London productions of "Peter Pan"—and was then chosen by Walt Disney for a major role in his film "The Prince and the Pauper."

She was also a frequent panellist on the BBC TV record review programme "Juke Box Jury," and with all these achievements behind her was already well-established by the time she met Paul McCartney on 9th May 1963. That day she had been asked to write a feature on The Beatles for the BBC programme magazine *Radio Times*. The Beatles spent the day rehearsing at the Royal Albert Hall for a major show that was to be broadcast on the BBC Light Programme that evening. During the afternoon there was a squabble over billing—because Del Shannon's British agent insisted what he should go on after The Beatles and close the show, which he did, enabling The Beatles to slip away from the hall to the Royal Court Hotel in Sloane Square where they were staying.

There they sat in the lounge drinking coffee and eating sandwiches with their manager Brian Epstein and over walked Jane Asher, asking if she could interview them for her article. Before she walked across, they had already decided to visit the nearby flat of a friend of mine, Chris Hutchins, who was then working as a journalist on the *New Musical Express* and who is now responsible for press and publicity for Tom Jones, Engelbert Humperdinck and Gilbert O' Sullivan.

As they left the hotel, Brian Epstein went back to the hotel where he was staying and Ringo stayed behind for an early night—and they all clambered into a large American car driven by a singer they had been appearing with earlier that day at the Albert Hall, Shane Fenton, now better known as Alvin Stardust. They drove along the Kings Road to Kings House, climbing three flights of stone steps to the top floor flat, with George Harrison making conversation with Jane.

At Hutchins' flat, the five men all sat on the floor, sitting in a circle with Jane in the middle as they turned the tables and started interviewing her for nearly two hours, seeking her view on any subject that came into their heads, and finishing off a bottle of whisky. Then after midnight Fenton said he would drive the three Beatles to a West End club he knew, dropping Jane off at her parents' home in Wimpole Street on the way. This they did—and as she got out of the car Paul asked if he could see her again. Having arranged to phone her, Paul joined John and George to drive on to the club—but when they arrived, they found it wasn't a club at all but a clip joint, with a hostess on the door demanding a thirty shilling admission fee, which Lennon thought was too much to pay, so the party broke up.

After that evening, Paul and Jane started seeing each other regularly, and their romance began—a romance that was to last over five years. It became public knowledge when they were recognised by fans waiting to see the show "Never Too Late" at the Prince of Wales Theatre; they were followed into the theatre, a flash bulb popped—and next day their photo was in the London daily papers. For the next five years, they issued constant denials of reports that they had either married, had arranged to marry, become engaged or fixed a date.

Unlike the wives of George Harrison, John Lennon and Ringo Starr, she pursued a very active career (George's wife Patti did continue with her modelling, but only to a limited degree). Jane had one of the star roles as Annie in the Michael Caine film "Alfie," appeared in the film "The Masque of the Red Death," appeared in TV serials like "The Saint," played Juliet in a TV production of "Romeo and Juliet," Maggie Tulliver in another TV production of George Eliot's "The Mill On The Floss" and Lise in "The Brothers Karamazov." Her stage appearances included Perdita in "A Winter's Tale" and Cassandra in "The Trojan Women;" the title role in "Cleo," a new play by Frank Marcus that was presented by the Bristol Old Vic Company, and the part of Ellen Terry in that company's production "Sixty Thousand Nights"; Eliza in "Pygmalion" at Watford, and many more. It was a career that developed quite separately from her relationship with McCartney. In 1967, they were apart for many months while she toured the States in the Bristol Old Vic production of "Romeo and Juliet"—appearing in Boston, Washington and Philadelphia—and McCartney flew out there to be with her on her 21st birthday.

Though her career was something to be proud of in itself, so far as the press were concerned it was her romance with Paul that was all-important. When they went on holiday together to the Portuguese fishing village of Albufeira, McCartney denied rumours that they had already married. "It is not true. Those things are never right," he said. When they were spotted by a journalist leaving the Comedy Theatre after seeing Spike Milligan in "Son of Oblomov," McCartney said: "When I marry, there will be none of this secrecy stuff. It just wouldn't work out." And when asked if they would marry, McCartney replied: "Just say that when you asked me this question, I smiled."

Throughout the years of his relationship with Jane Asher, his life was quite different to that of the other Beatles. He enjoyed living right in the heart of London. His mind was growingly receptive, and a little self-consciously he told *Disc and Music Echo* that he was on a programme of "self-improvement and education," and to the London *Evening Standard* he said: "I don't want to sound like Jonathan Miller going on, but I'm trying to cram everything in, all the things that I've missed. People are saying things and painting things and writing things and composing things that are great, and I must know what people are doing."

He became more political, though not as publicly so as John Lennon later did; he was not afraid to admit quite publicly that he had experimented with the drug LSD, and neither did he shy away from questions about his religious beliefs. McCartney was born and brought up a Roman Catholic, and appears never to have totally lost his religious beliefs—when he and Linda later married after the

57

civil ceremony they went round to a church in St. John's Wood to be blessed.

Partly, I suspect this candour was all part of a general feeling of relaxation that he appears to have felt as he organised his domestic arrangements; he appeared to have acquired a sense of direction and control that the others had not—which showed itself when he quickly started trying to organise their affairs after Epstein's death.

Tony Barrow, who had been associated with The Beatles from the very beginning saw this as clearly as anyone. It was while Barrow was writing a record review column for the Liverpool evening paper under the pen-name "Disker" that Epstein wrote to him, having recently met The Beatles for the first time, and asked if he could suggest ways of them being given a recording test; Barrow subsequently arranged their test with Decca, who turned them down early in 1962, but Epstein never forgot the kindness—and when The Beatles needed a full-time publicist the following year Epstein gave the job to Barrow. He told *The Telegraph* Colour Supplement: "Paul is now leading a very organised life. The other three don't know what they are doing. They wait for others to tell them. But Paul always knows—you ring him up and he will say, 'No, not Thursday, I am dining at eight. No—Friday, because I have got to see a man about a painting. But Saturday's okay.' It isn't that he's changed. But out of all of them he has developed the most."

As the months and years passed, and the whole craziness of the years of Beatlemania faded away, it became possible for Paul McCartney to move about quite normally—he had already developed several disguises (which ranged from false beards to grubby old raincoats, tattered hats and glasses) and prided himself on being able to board a bus from Liverpool to Chester without anyone knowing who he was. Once he and Jane Asher even went on a safari holiday to Kenya without being recognised—because on that occasion he grew a moustache and had his hair cut almost to a stubble by the stylist Leslie Cavendish from Vidal Sassoon.

But as time moved on, even the disguises became

largely unnecessary. In the evenings he had always been able to move from club to club without being harassed, occasionally he would dine out at lunch-time, go shopping, walk his sheepdog Martha in Regents Park most mornings without being troubled, and on those occasions when someone came up to him and asked, "You're not Paul Mc-Cartney, are you?" he soon found that all he had to say was either, "Who? Me!" or "People are always saying that"—and the people concerned would just walk away, looking either puzzled or a little embarrassed.

Part of the secret was that he and Jane could vanish whenever they wanted to; that large home he bought in St. John's Wood, with enormous walls around the garden and electronically controlled gates, gave him almost total seclusion right in the heart of London—and when he really wanted to get away he could either drive or fly to his farm, which was as private as anyone could hope to be. The lives he began to lead in the two homes were quite different.

In London, his town house reflected his status as part of the city's new aristocracy; it was secluded, yet right in the heart of London with every facility he needed so that he could stay for days there if he wanted to without ever having to go out, knowing that everyone—be they tailor or shirtmaker, hair stylist or accountant—would come to him if he wanted to see them.

It is a large, spacious house, deep carpeted in dark browns and grey with many rugs scattered loosely, but not furnished either tastelessly or with too much attention to fashion. One thing visitors frequently noticed was that an old fashioned table cloth invariable covered the living room table which is an ingrained social habit if ever there was one; I can remember from childhood how Northern families invariably had their living room table thus so that it could be an all-purpose part of the home. In fact, much of McCartney's furniture he bought cheaply secondhand and restored himself, giving each room character with treasures picked up in junk or antique shops—like his collection of very early sheet music, the clock from the Great Exhibition of 1851, a Paolozzi sculpture called "Solo," those Tiffany lampshades or his collection of Beatles souvenirs (though most of those are still lying upstairs in their packing cases in any empty room—and many of his gold and silver discs adorn the walls of his father's home at Heswall, Cheshire).

With its three bathrooms, guest bedrooms, separate quarters for the couple who then looked after him (he and Linda now have help during the day but the house to themselves in the evenings), with a vast modern kitchen and well stocked stores the house could be—and sometimes became—almost a little world of its own, with a music room where he could write, using a whole range of different instruments, and a workshop where he could potter. Essentially he was also at the heart of things—with two phones (whose numbers had to be changed constantly), with the Nems and other music business offices, the West End theatres and cinemas, and EMI's and the other London recording studios only a matter of minutes away. It was and is a well organised life, leaving him able to enjoy the life of a city sophisticate.

In contrast, the life he created for himself in Scotland was much more spartan. There he would swap his Aston Martin for a Land Rover and wearing jeans, old T-shirts, sweaters or a wind cheater jacket stride through the heather amongst his sheep on the wind-beaten hills overlooking the Mull of Kintyre, with his old English Sheepdog Martha ambling along at his side. The contrast could hardly be more marked; the first farm he bought, High Park, near Machrihanish, with its 183 acres of land, lies at the end of a lane four and a half miles long, and even when you get to the end of that lane the McCartney homestead can only be reached by crossing another farmer's land—and farmer John MacDougall became a sufficiently good friend to make sure that very few visitors crossed it. In winter, the lanes up to the high, exposed, bleak farm often became almost impassable because of snow; at other times of the year McCartney would either work on the farm—he employs a couple there to look after the land for him while he is away—or would sometimes drive into the nearest town, Campbeltown, in his Land Rover to collect groceries, to see how much his sheep fetched at market, or sometimes even to pop into a local dance, thus soon becoming accepted as part of the local community.

This was a strangely fragmented life-style that he had developed during the time that he and Jane Asher were together. His large home like an oasis in the heart of London enabled him to carry on with his work as a musician and as a part of The Beatles; the constant relationship that be maintained with his family in Heswall and Cheshire and Liverpool—and his totally different way of life in one of the remotest parts of Scotland. (More recently it has become even more varied with his decision to have another home specially built for him in Sardinia and with his frequent holidays either in Jamaica or with Linda's family in New York, with working holidays using different studios in places as far apart as Nashville, New Orleans, Lagos and the West Indies.) All this could hardly be more different to the life he had known in childhood and through his teens in Liverpool, moving from one council estate to another—or, indeed, to his early days as one of The Beatles.

The fact that he had so many bolt-holes and could move between them by privately hired jet when he wanted to meant that Paul McCartney could—and did—disappear from public view for weeks and even months on end, with only his closest friends, personal staff and family knowing where he was. Because of this some quite bizarre rumours started to circulate about him in the States and even in Britain in the mid-to-late Sixties before he started being seen more frequently again after his marriage to Linda Eastman.

Twice rumours swept the United States that he was in fact dead, and to support that belief a series of very strange myths developed around McCartney and his relationship with the other Beatles. It was rumoured that the symbolism in one of the tracks on the "Sgt. Pepper" album—the track "A Day In The Life"—was a reference to his own death by the other Beatles, and that it was really he who "blew his mind out in a car." It was suggested that what appeared to be a grave on the sleeve design of that same LP was also a reference to McCartney's

61

death—as was the floral wreath that lay on the same grave.

Likewise, it was later said that there was great significance in the "Abbey Road" album sleeve—because Ringo appeared to be dressed as an undertaker, George Harrison as a gravedigger and John Lennon as a clergyman with Paul in a normal suit, but walking barefoot. For the sleuths discovered that in Italy bare feet were the mark of a corpse! And then the everwatchful ghouls noticed that the parked Volkswagen photographed on the same LP sleeve had the numberplate "281F"—which was taken to mean that Paul McCartney would have been *28 IF* he had lived.

Then it was noticed that the letters "OPD" appeared on an armband in another LP sleeve photograph of Paul— and that was taken to mean that he was "Officially Pronounced Dead." In another photo he was seen to be wearing a black flower while the other three Beatles all had red flowers—and that was said to be another sign. All in all, the rumours circulated for around three years between 1966 and 1969, with suggestions that he had been decapitated in a road accident in November, 1966, and that The Beatles, for financial reasons, had decided to keep his death a secret. It was even reported in the London *Evening News* that there were rumours to the effect that The Beatles had replaced him with a double, whose real name was William Campbell, who had been given plastic surgery to complete the illusion.

Repeated in print like this, the whole series of rumours sound quite absurd—which, of course, they were. But for quite some time during his relationship with Jane Asher, Paul McCartney made no attempt to re-appear in public— because he saw no reason why he should. And when he eventually did, on both occasions that the rumours had reached their heights, it was only to suggest that if he really was dead perhaps people would tell him first!

After the last live appearance by The Beatles at Candlestick Park, San Francisco, in August 1966, Paul McCartney was only seen when he turned up in the audience for a new play or film in the West End; when he made films with Lennon, Harrison and Starr to promote their new singles and albums because as well as ceasing to make live stage appearances. The Beatles also gradually withdrew from TV studio appearances, too, producing their own film instead and offering it to TV companies in Britain and around the world, and when he and they might give a series of interviews to a few selected journalists—mainly from the music papers—again to promote some new project.

Through those years he and Jane Asher were inseparable, often staying at his father's home near Liverpool, going to family weddings and other celebrations, dining, catching most of the important London theatrical productions, seeing each other work (she would quite often join him when he was working, and he would make a point of seeing all her plays and TV productions). From the magazine articles that had appeared fans thought they knew everything about her—that she spoke fluent French and some Russian, played classical guitar, was an accomplished cook, and widely read. And because she was so publicly associated with Paul McCartney, she was resented by many fans—who started sending her anonymous letters threatening to injure her, throw acid in her face, burn her hair, and so on. She even received phone calls threatening murder. Although she and McCartney tried to avoid publicity, and avoided answering questions about their relationship the speculation was intense.

"I don't need the publicity," Jane told the *Sunday Express*. "I don't want it—and I don't like it. It puts me at such an awful disadvantage, you know . . . it upsets me and I hate being upset. Because when I'm upset I'm no good at my work or anything. And this puts me at a disadvantage. I know that most people say that basically I love it all, and am secretly overjoyed and revelling in the gossip. But they're wrong. They just don't understand about actresses and the theatre . . . I've become a publicity freak, and this I resent. How do I begin to tell you what it means to an actress who's trying to make it on talent alone?"

On "The Eamonn Andrews Show" on ITV, Jane said they were "not married, engaged or thinking about getting married—I'm just his girlfriend"; to *The Sunday Mirror* she said: "No, I am not Paul's wife—but yes, we are going to get married . . . we won't be married for a while yet, but when it happens we've got a family planned. First we want a boy and then—come what may. There's no particular reason why we are not getting married right away, except that we're both pretty young . . . I shan't give up my career unless it interferes with our being together," and to *The Daily Express* she said: "I love Paul. I love him very deeply, and he feels the same. I don't think either of us has looked at anyone else since we first met . . . we would just like to be alone. I want to get married, probably this year (1967), and have lot and lots of babies. I certainly would be very surprised indeed if I married anyone but Paul . . . we won't be getting married in America or anything like that. I want our wedding to be in England with my family and everyone there."

Together, they had seemed to be preparing themselves for the marriage; they had chosen the furnishings together for Paul's house in St. John's Wood; together they had looked over the farm near Campbeltown that had become his country home, furnishing that together, too. Over Christmas, 1967, they told their respective families that they were now formally engaged—and on Christmas Day itself Paul gave her an emerald and diamond ring. A few months later they both attended his brother Michael's wedding . . . and then suddenly it was all over.

First of all Paul surprised his friends by turning up alone for the premiere of the "Yellow Submarine" cartoon film, and then a few days later Jane appeared alone on the BBC TV programme "Dee Time," and told its host Simon Dee: "It's finished . . . I don't really want to talk about it." When Dee suggested that she had broken off the engagement, Jane replied: "I haven't broken it off . . ." Later she told the Sunday press that she did not want to say any more—and as soon as the programme finished Paul left his home in St. John's Wood and drove north to spend the weekend with his father. "Paul has never given any hint that he and Jane were parting," said Mr. McCartney.

"They were a really happy couple at their engagement party last Christmas . . ."

For some days there was speculation that this might be just a temporary rift but soon Paul was seen around the London clubs with other girls—one of whom, Francie Schwartz, told her story to the *News of The World*. She said she had moved into the house. "He hadn't formally ended his friendship with Jane Asher, so at first I was a secret. Sometimes the phone rang. It was easy to tell when Jane was on the other end. Paul would get very uptight, very awkward," she said. In *The People*, McCartney was reported to have holidayed in Sardinia with another girl, Maggie McGivern.

And then another girl came into his life . . . Linda Eastman.

Chapter Five

The relationship that Paul McCartney had and still has with the other Beatles and which they all had with Brian Epstein has been the subject of intense speculation—most of it ill-founded. John Lennon, George Harrison, Ringo Starr and Paul McCartney were in the beginning and still are far more business-like and professional in their approach to their work as musicians than their audience has ever been given cause to suspect—for the best of reasons.

It is another of those strange music business myths, which The Beatles and Epstein observed as much as anyone else, that artistes should never talk about their money. There were very good reasons for this back in the early Sixties; not much money was being made by the different groups of the time, but they were all very conscious that it was far more than their fans could ever hope to earn—and that they might very easily become disenchanted if they ever realised just how commercial an industry pop music was becoming. There was another very good reasons, too; musicians are not fools—and they know that there is a department within the Inland Revenue that takes all the music papers and combs them for information about stars' earnings. Thus, for a variety of reasons, the tradition developed that money like marriage was something that pop stars never discussed; to do so was thought to be the kiss of death.

So if a Beatle ever talked about Epstein, it was in terms of friendship—to say how much they owed to his guidance, how they enjoyed his company, how he was just like one of them—and that was all nonsense. He was not like one of them at all. He was a kind man, attentive in small details, quick to give personal gifts—but this was something that developed as their careers progressed.

He was really nothing more than a business man of middling ability who happened to have been in the right place at the right time—and the simple truth is that The Beatles could still have made it without Brian Epstein, but Brian Epstein would never have made it without The Beatles. There were hundreds of other businessmen who could have done what he did—and it's quite probable that they would not have made some of the mistakes he made. Some of the contracts that he signed in the early days were very foolish—and he was tempted more than once to sell his interest in The Beatles. As a failed drama student, he had a latent interest in the Arts—which probably explains why he was prepared to take some risks in the very beginning. The fact that he was a homosexual, though in itself not necessarily anything to be ashamed of, probably explains why he found it difficult to establish relationships with people.

Even when they first met him, The Beatles treated him with caution—they always had a healthy suspicion of businessmen. At their first interview, Paul McCartney did not even bother to turn up on time—but had a bath instead. And when they were invited to meet him again to sign their first contract, John Lennon took along the Liverpool disc jockey Bob Wooler as an independent witness—and when Epstein asked who he was, Lennon grunted: "It's me Dad!" Much later when Epstein tried to give them advice on recording a particular song, Lennon told him quite bluntly to leave the music to them—and just count the percentages!

What was different about Epstein was his social background. Whereas The Beatles were all from working class families, and were themselves tough characters who would occasionally settle disputes with their fists (one eyewitness told me that one of their fights at the Star Club in Hamburg lasted nearly two hours), Epstein himself was from a middle class family, educated at public school, always conventionally dressed, short-haired and clean-shaven—every bit the young company director rising in the family business without having to struggle too hard. To put it crudely, he knew how to behave. When The Beatles and he first met, from what he once told me himself, from what he says in his autobiography and from other published comments, their reaction towards him would seem to have been a mixture of awe, respect and suspicion. And I don't think I am doing either him or them an injustice in saying that this was something that never quite left their relationship—though even they were probably unaware in the very early days that the first contract he signed was not valid because Epstein (keeping his options open) had not signed his part of the agreement.

Indeed, by his own behaviour Epstein seemed to accentuate the distance between them. He put their relationship on a firmly businesslike basis—unlike many of today's managers who have a deeply personal day-by-day relationship with their artistes, Esptein would often leave The Beatles to make TV appearances, to travel off to concerts and even to tour overseas without accompanying them himself. Minor problems that arose would be dealt with by their road managers Neil Aspinall and Malcolm Evans—while Epstein would stay in his office working or perhaps guiding another of his artistes. When The Beatles first came down to London in 1963, Epstein would stay in an expensive hotel in Park Lane, Mayfair—while The Beatles were booked into much cheaper accommodation in Russell Square.

Likewise, the relationships between The Beatles themselves was more professional than the public image suggested. For the first nine or ten months of their relationship with Epstein there was a different drummer, Pete Best—and I can remember Neil Aspinall telling me that when their recording manager George Martin suggested that Pete Best had to go, The Beatles made it quite plain to Epstein that that was a job for him to do and not them. Initially, Ringo was very much on trial—and was more than a little shaken when he turned up for one recording session and found another drummer sitting there at the drum kit, a session musician brought in by George Martin for the occasion. Indeed for some months after he joined Ringo did not even know that John Lennon was married.

Thus, although Paul and John had been friends since 1955 and although they had known George Harrison since 1958, there was a distinctly taut relationship both within The Beatles and in their separate and collective relationships with Epstein, and until one understands this and the implications of it one cannot put all their achievements in their right perspective. It is true that The Beatles eventually started calling Epstein "Eppy"—and that as time went by he made a considerable effort to bridge the gap between them. To a large extent, he succeeded—but the relationship was still fundamentally business-like. To give him his due, The Beatles had far more say in the way their career progressed than most groups did; as well as writing their music and playing it they also participated in nearly every major business decision—and when Epstein was tempted to accept one particular offer to buy him out it was they who talked him out of it. It is difficult to be wholly accurate in describing a series of complex personal relationships, but at the time I knew several people who were very close to Epstein. Quite often after he had spent a night gambling or at a dinner I would hear verbatim accounts of what he had said during the evening, and there were people within The Beatles' immediate entourage who would often drop in at my flat for supper or to play chess—and from all this it became very clear that individually Lennon, Harrison, McCartney and Starr were leading very separate lives and their meetings with Epstein, though friendly and increasingly based on a mutual trust, nevertheless had a distinctly formal edge to them.

Those earliest offers to buy Epstein out were never publicised at the time, though I do know who the offers were from and how much they were for (the highest was £250,000). From 1964 onwards, when The Beatles were a world-wide "property" he had even more offers—though as late as the autumn of 1966 he described reports that Allen Klein had been approached by two of The Beatles as "ridiculous." What is important to remember is that as the

years slipped by, Epstein had little, then nothing, to sell
. . . his contract with The Beatles was running out.

Now I am not for one moment suggesting that The Beatles had decided to break away from Epstein—but it was widely believed in the music business at the time that Epstein himself was very much afraid that it might happen.

In my own files, I have a photocopy of the second contract that The Beatles signed with Epstein—after he had formed Nems Enterprises Ltd., and after Ringo Starr had replaced Pete Best. That photocopy is on my desk now, and the contract was dated 1st October, 1962, and was due to run for a period of five years "provided always that either party to this Agreement may terminate this Agreement by giving 3 months notice in writing to the other party by registered post at his or their last known address to expire on the anniversary of each year of this Agreement . . ."

The contract was signed by all four Beatles, and also by Paul's father and George's father because they were both under the age of contractual consent when it was first signed. It was a fairly stiff contract giving Epstein and Nems control of most aspects of The Beatles' professional work—and *twenty five per cent* of their income (though had they each earned less than £100 a week Nems would only have received fifteen percent, and had their individual income been less than £200 a week Nems would only have received twenty per cent). This was a higher percentage than most artistes paid their managers.

For the first years of that contract, The Beatles worked at a very hard pace (the details can be seen in the appendix); they toured Britain frequently, made three major nationwide tours of the United States, visited most countries in Europe, toured Australia, New Zealand and Japan; they made the first two films under their three-film contract with United Artists, "A Hard Day's Night" and "Help!"—and in the months that preceded Brian Epstein's death I know of no evidence to suggest that they were then planning not to continue the general direction their career was taking. They had long had a feeling that their recording sessions had been too rushed, and that they would prefer to spend more time recording each album—and there was also a general feeling within the group that they would like to try solo projects.

Thus in the autumn of 1966, John Lennon made his first solo film appearance in "How I Won The War"; George Harrison started studying Indian music; Paul McCartney became the first member of the group to write a film score (for "The Family Way"), and after they had all had a holiday they produced the "Penny Lane"/ "Strawberry Fields" single and began working at a far more leisurely pace on the next album "Sgt. Pepper's Lonely Hearts Club Band." This album showed just how much better they could be when they had the time to put that extra work into it. Before the album was released, they signed a new nine-year contract with EMI . . . but their contract with Epstein still had a few months to run. And then, before a new contract was ever signed, he died.

Of course, they were upset by his death; Epstein was as close to them as any business colleague could be—but without in any way trying to be callous I think this was the moment when the fact that his relationship with them had been so businesslike really showed itself. Outwardly, they appeared to recover quickly; a fortnight after his death they went ahead with the "Magical Mystery Tour" film—which McCartney produced himself (and which I personally believe to have been a far more successful project than the TV critics ever understood). It has often been suggested that the other members of the group resented the fact that McCartney tended to take a more dominating influence in their affairs at that time—but it is as well to remember that there always had been a certain amount of ego-conflict within The Beatles. Indeed, this is true of most groups—there have been some world-famous acts whose internal relationships have been a dreadful mess; some have never spoken to each other apart from when they have been working. After the initial excitement of moving down to London—when Epstein had found them a flat to share in Green Street, Mayfair, after they had had enough of living in hotel rooms—The Beatles had all gone their separate ways.

72

Lennon had brought his wife Cynthia and son Julian down from Liverpool, where they had been living with his Aunt Mimi, and moved into a house in Weybridge. Ringo had married Maureen and moved to Weybridge, and George Harrison had moved to Esher and married Patti, McCartney continuing his relationship with Jane Asher. With their wives and families and personal friends, they all had separate lives of their own—and though they would quite often make up foursomes, go to each other's homes or bring their wives down to the studios, they would also often go long periods without seeing each other.

Even the stories about the Lennon-McCartney songwriting partnership were largely a myth, hatched early in 1963 when Epstein had been trying—very sensibly—to bring out the personality of each member of the group. I can remember him saying that he was anxious that they should each receive comparable amounts of publicity, and not become one of those groups where the singer was the star and the backing group almost anonymous. In fact, Lennon and McCartney, though they were the main songwriters in the group, wrote together only rarely—and theirs was not a partnership in the traditional Hollywood movie sense of two songwriters always sitting down at a piano to write their songs (though they did obligingly pose for some photographs at a piano together) and the music papers maintained the myth by always talking about Lennon-McCartney compositions even when they knew that certain songs had been written by either one or the other. This is described in some detail in chapter seven.

In managerial terms, this was one of Epstein's great achievements; all four members of The Beatles became individual stars—and by the time he died they were four very individual people, each acutely aware of his own talent, each highly ambitious, and each with his own ideas of what he and the group should do next.

At the same time, they had bred a monster—The Beatles had become the most successful phenomenon in the history of Entertainment; both in audience and financial terms they were bigger than Elvis Presley, Frank Sinatra or any of the cinema greats like Marilyn Monroe or Clark Gable.

And they knew it.

They said at the time that it would be impossible for anyone to take over from Epstein. And because the contract with Nems was running out, that presented no problem. At the same time, I suspect they also knew that The Beatles could not continue quite as they were—that last American tour had been a nightmare with Ku Klux Klansmen picketing one hall, high explosive firecrackers being thrown at them on stage, and at some venues cripples being wheeled into wherever they were standing for them to touch (which they had found quite sickening).

There was no argument about making "Magical Mystery Tour"; that went ahead quite normally—as did their recording sessions, their filming of promotional film clips, their interviews and photo sessions, all timed to tie in with each new project.

If they did make a mistake, it was the quite understandable one of thinking they could do it all themselves. After all, it was they who had taken most of the crucial decisions in their time with Epstein—but what they appeared not to realise was that there is all the difference in the world between actually taking a decision and being the person who has to implement that decision, to negotiate its consequences and take public responsibility for it. It was the old, old story of the lawyer who represents himself having a fool for a client.

Their motives could not have been finer. They launched Apple, provided opportunities for their friends in Liverpool who had not had the breaks they had had—planned to use the vast fortune that they were accumulating to encourage creative talent in every branch of the performing and creative Arts. This they did with great success—setting up their offices in a Georgian block in Savile Row, London, that they bought for £500,000, and recruiting a staff of nearly forty people. There they established one of the best recording studios in London. Their record label is still one of the most successful in the world—and through it Mary Hopkin, Badfinger and James Taylor besides each

74

of The Beatles with their own successful solo projects have all reached an international audience.

At one time, they launched their own boutique (which was intended to be the first in a chain), talked of forming a chain of clubs, financed a children's theatre group, started planning a school for their own and other stars' children, patented electronic inventions, put promising songwriters on a retainer—and were generally a soft touch for anyone with a bright idea and a good line in patter.

If one visited Apple, as I did occasionally, there was a permanent light show running in one of the offices; apparently unlimited sources of booze—and an atmosphere of creative mayhem. Although all four Beatles threw themselves into Apple with great enthusiasm—and McCartney himself had considerable success recording and writing for Mary Hopkin—administratively Apple became a mess. Some years later, after McCartney had issued his High Court writ to formally dissolve The Beatles' partnership, John Lennon said in an affidavit to the Court that Apple had become full of "spongers" and "hustlers" and that "the staff came and went as they pleased and were lavish with money and hospitality. We have since discovered that at around that time two of Apple's cars had completely disappeared, and we also owned a house which no-one can remember buying . . ."

At one stage, Lennon and McCartney were reported to have had a meeting with Lord Beeching, asking him to come in and handle their administrative affairs. After he had met Linda Eastman, McCartney suggested that her father and brother—who were and are two of America's top show business lawyers—might take over and then the other members of The Beatles insisted on appointing Allen Klein as business manager, although McCartney strongly opposed the decision.

Klein was appointed, and it is only fair to him to say that he does have an extraordinary reputation within the music business for being the "doctor" to be brought in when musicians have doubts about their contracts; he would go along to record companies, check their accounts, make sure that all the royalties have been paid, and cross-check all his finds. Some of his coups have become legendary, though for the reasons that I have already mentioned in this book these have not been publicised—but he is certainly reputed to have "earned" musicians hundreds of thousands of pounds that they might otherwise never have received. Equally it is only fair to say that he did subsequently re-negotiate The Beatles' contract with EMI, earning them a very much increased royalty. Nevertheless McCartney was violently opposed to his appointment, and nearly two years passed before McCartney finally took the dispute to Court—two years during which most of the rows that he had with the others were unknown outside their immediate circle.

They became publicised only when the case went to Court, and affidavits by John Lennon, George Harrison and Ringo Starr were read. In his affidavit, John Lennon said there had always been a lot of arguing within the group, mainly over musical matters when they were touring. "I suppose Paul and George were the main offenders but from time to time we all gave displays of temperament and threatened to walk out. Of necessity, we developed a pattern for sorting out our differences by doing what any three of us decided," said Lennon. "It sometimes took a long time and sometimes there was deadlock and nothing was done . . . (but) it generally worked quite well."

Lennon said of Klein: "I wanted him as my manager. I introduced him to the other three. But if Paul is trying to suggest that I was rushing them and pushing him down their throats, this is a wrong impression. I thought that Paul would agree with us in the end after he had seen the benefit of Klein's work. I would have liked him to have agreed with us before the ABKCO (Klein's company) agreement was signed, but I thought he was being unreasonable towards the other three of us, and knew that in the last resort his signature was not necessary. So far as I am concerned Paul did accept Klein as The Beatles manager, though he may not have liked him. I remember Klein being very hurt when after he had flown from New York to London at Paul's and my request, Paul later completely changed his tune and refused to co-operate with us . . .

Paul's criticisms of Klein may reflect his dislike of the man but I don't think they are fair. Klein is certainly forceful to an extreme but he does get results. He doesn't sow discord between us . . . royalties are coming in in greater sums than they ever were before Klein started to re-organise The Beatles' affairs."

Of The Eastmans, Lennon said: "John Eastman gave me the impression of being an inexperienced and somewhat excitable and easily confused young man . . . Lee Eastman was more impressive at first sight, but after about five minutes' conversation he lost his temper and became quite hysterical, screaming and shouting abuse at Klein."

Lennon also said that he thought McCartney was being "wise after the event" in saying that in 1968 musical differences between them had become more marked and that the group were beginning to drift apart. "From our earliest days in Liverpool, George and I on the one hand and Paul on the other had different musical tastes. Paul preferred 'pop type' music and we preferred what is now called 'underground'. This may have led to arguments, particularly between Paul and George, but the contrast in our tastes, I am sure, did more good than harm musically speaking and contributed to our success." And of a suggestion by McCartney that Lennon had been no longer interested in performing songs he had not written himself, John Lennon said it was "greatly exaggerated. The boot was on the other foot. George and Ringo tell me that we were each as bad as the other in that respect and that it was no worse then than in the past years."

In his affidavit, Ringo Starr said that Paul McCartney was "the greatest bass guitar player in the world. He is also very determined. He goes on and on to see if he can get his own way. While that may be a virtue, it did mean that musical disagreements inevitably arose from time to time. But such disagreements contributed to really great products." Of John Eastman, Ringo said: "He did not seem to me to be cut out to enjoy dealing with the hurly-burly of business life or to relish the pretty tough world of the music scene. Klein impressed me straight away. He took the trouble to find out what he could do about our problems."

77

Ringo referred to one of the disputes that had happened within the group in recent years—when McCartney wanted to release his first solo album, "McCartney," but that the timing for this was regarded by the others as being in conflict with the release date for their "Let It Be" album and Ringo's own solo album "Sentimental Journey." "I went to see Paul. To my dismay, he went completely out of control, shouting at me, prodding his fingers towards my face, saying: 'I'll finish you now' and 'You'll pay' . . . he told me to put my coat on and get out. I did so," said Ringo. "While I thought that Paul had behaved like a spoiled child, I could see that the release date of his record had a gigantic emotional significance for him. Whether he was right or wrong, I felt that since he was our friend and that the date was of such immense significance to him, we should let him have his own way. So I persuaded the others and with some difficulty my release was put forward two weeks and the group's 'Let It Be' was put back."

In his affidavit, George Harrison said that there had been a major row while they were filming "Let It Be." He said that McCartney had always shown a superior attitude towards his (Harrison's) music. "To get a peaceful life I had always let him have his own way even when it meant that songs I had composed were not being recorded but at the same time I was having to record his songs and put up with him telling me how to play my own instrument . . . (on the 'Let It Be' film) we were actually in front of the cameras. Paul started to get at me about the way I was playing. I decided I had had enough and I told the others I was leaving the group."

Another dispute that was mentioned in Court was over the film itself. McCartney said it had been sold to United Artists without his knowledge—and he also complained that on one of his own tracks on the "Let It Be" album, "The Long and Winding Road," extra voices and instruments had been added to the track without his knowledge, which his counsel told the Court McCartney saw as "a serious threat to his artistic freedom and his freedom to exploit his artistic talents."

There was much discussion in the Court over The Beatles' finances—and even Paul's one solo album up to that date, "McCartney," was said to have already earned £487,000 in royalties—and at the end of the eleven-day hearing McCartney's request was met. A Receiver was appointed, and Klein was removed from office—though the Judge stressed that there was no evidence at all that Klein had pocketed any of The Beatles' money. But he said that McCartney had solid grounds for mistrusting him. "However successful Mr. Klein may have been in generating income, I am satisfied on the accounts that the financial situation is confused, uncertain and inconclusive," said Mr. Justice Stamp. He also said: "The appointment of ABKCO, without the concurrence of Paul, was, in my judgement, a breach of the terms of the partnership deed . . ."

The publication of the affidavits and the evidence as to The Beatles' finances—which disclosed an income of £17,500,000 in eight and a half years *without their songwriting income*—was the first that most of the fans could ever have heard of the disputes that had racked the group for years. But, as I have mentioned earlier in this book, disputes were nothing new—and as I stressed in the first chapter for all his tremendous personal charm, his talent, his ingenuity and diplomatic skill, Paul McCartney was and is a very tough operator. But then so were all four Beatles—both in the early days, in their years with Epstein, during the period when they were launching Apple, and then later when they saw their interests conflicting. The image that developed around them of four carefree, happy-go-lucky "mop tops" could hardly have been more absurd.

They were and are tough and ambitious, prepared to work far harder than most people would ever think possible, possessed of extraordinary self-confidence—and the belief that their music, both individually and collectively, is important. And they also have the capacity which few people do of being able to compromise, find areas of agreement—and then move on—which is why it was no surprise to me to learn that Lennon, Harrison and Starr had themselves broken with Klein, started their own proceedings against him, and that even after the bitterness of the High Court proceedings, the rows which preceded it, and the angry Lennon attack on McCartney in his song "How Do You Sleep?", they had still come back together again socially.

Their fans never realised it, but there had been many violent rows in the past—each member of the group had at one time or another threatened to walk out. And even at the time that Paul said he had left The Beatles, John Lennon thought that *he* had left first. What was so different about the dispute that led to the High Court case was that it was about an outsider—and once he had gone, McCartney started meeting the others again socially and for business meetings, and even wrote a track specially for one of Ringo's solo albums.

It has even been rumoured that three of them (and maybe even all four) have worked together again in the privacy of a recording studio, and it is now widely believed within the music business itself that they will eventually record together, though possibly not until after February, 1976, when their nine-year contract with EMI expires. John Lennon, Paul McCartney and Ringo Starr have all hinted at this—though there does seem to be still an antagonism between McCartney and George Harrison, which is musical rather than personal.

But they have always overcome feelings of this kind in the past, and my own belief is that this is precisely what they will do now, since they all realise that reuniting musically would give an enormous boost to their different solo projects.

Chapter Six

By the time they met, Linda Eastman had a background
that was as complicated as Paul McCartney's, though in
different ways. She came from a wealthy family and had
been brought up in a very exclusive part of New York,
Scarsdale, living in a beautiful home surrounded by fine
furniture and rare paintings. Her father, Lee Eastman, is
an art collector; her mother was killed in a plane crash. It
may be because of her wealth that Linda was widely reported to be related to the Eastmans who made a vast fortune from film, cinema and photographic products—the
Kodak-Eastman empire which included products ranging
from tiny rolls of camera film to the Eastmancolour process by which many of Hollywood's top movies are produced. But she has been quoted as denying that this is
true; certainly both her father, Lee, and her brother, John,
are lawyers, advising many internationally famous show
business clients—which was their work long before she met
Paul McCartney. (Peter Evans, a British show business
writer, has written that the family name was originally Epstein—and was changed to Eastman by her father.)

"I grew up used to seeing people like Tommy Dorsey,
Hoagy Carmichael, Hopalong Cassidy and Harold Arlen
around the house," Linda once told me, adding that the
very normality of it all, with them sitting down at the dinner table or in the lounge, meant that show business people had never seemed anything other than ordinary people
to her. "Show business always seemed to me to be a quite
normal way for people to earn their living," she said,

though the fact that she thought this meant the idea of working in the business herself was one that never entered her head.

As a child, she says she was always restless, always anxious to know what life was like outside the rather exclusive, privileged world in which she lived, and she describes herself as being the "black sheep of the family" because her parents really didn't know what to make of her and she didn't know what she wanted to make of her own life. The one thing that she was very aware of was an attitude in the family home, a feeling that was passed down to her, that life was very competitive, and that you had to work harder and try harder than the next person if you were ever going to make much progress.

"I was forced to learn piano," she said when I asked what were the earliest musical influences she had, "and like a lot of children forced to do something against their will, I rebelled against that, learnt nothing—and finally got my way. I'm sorry now, of course, because it would be nice to have had that grounding. Now I've started all over again."

From school she went on to University, studying art and history; married for the first time, gave birth to her daughter, Heather (who has since been legally adopted by Paul), though the marriage had broken up four years before she met McCartney.

"When my marriage broke up, I decided to get away from everything I had ever known before," she told me, "and I moved down to Tucson, Arizona, with Heather, staying with friends, studying photography at a local college, and spending much of my time riding on the edge of the desert . . . for the first time I started going round with artists, actors and writers, and all that helped me to discover who I am. It changed my life, meeting so many interesting, intelligent people . . . "

Before that, she had never been involved in rock music, though at school in the late Fifties she used to listen to Alan Freed's radio show, which played many of the early rhythm 'n' blues records, and early rock 'n' roll. The first record that she can remember really being impressed by was The Platters' track 'Earth Angel'. "After that, whenever I should have been doing my school homework I'd always be listening to Chuck Berry, Buddy Holly and Jerry Lee Lewis, and I'd always rather be doing that than anything else . . . whenever my parents wanted me to go out anywhere with them, I'd never want to go because I was quite happy staying at home or driving around in the car, just listening to the radio. Music has always been there for me in a very big way."

After living in Arizona, she eventually returned to New York, by now interested in photography, and having bought herself a Pentax. "I've never been a mechanically minded photographer," she explained to me. "That first course I went on down in Tucson was a disappointment because when I went along to the college I found it was more of an artistic course, concentrating also on photographers' lives . . . I wasn't too keen on that, but it stimulated my interest in photography, and I started taking a lot of pictures, using my intuition over things like light and exposure . . . I got myself a job on *Town and Country Magazine,* which is sort of society fashion magazine and not what you'd think from its title, and after I'd been there a few months they decided to feature a cover on The Rolling Stones, and I was sent along to do the job . . . The Stones were on a yacht, and all the other photographers were hustled off the boat, and I found myself the only one left on the boat, so I started taking millions of pictures . . . when I got off this boat, there were all these journalists and photographers who hadn't been able to get the photos I'd got so they asked to use my pictures instead, and that got my name around . . . that was a great piece of luck, and I left my job and started freelancing."

She specialised in rock photos, seeing all the visiting British musicians, attending press conferences and photocalls, and getting them alone for exclusive photos when she could. "The people I tried to concentrate on were those whose music I liked, because I think you have to identify with people," she said. "That way you can keep up a conversation while you're working, and that develops a relationship that puts them at their ease, and that way you get better pictures . . . the great thing about my sessions was

83

that musicians found they could relax because I would be chattering away about music, and they would know that I loved the music, and out of it came some great pictures."

It was through her work that she first met Paul McCartney, having flown to London in 1967 for a photo-session with Steve Winwood's group Traffic; she stayed on a few days, and one evening was taken down to the Bag O'Nails by Chas Chandler to see Georgie Fame and the Blue Flames. (Formerly bass player with the Animals, Chandler discovered Jimi Hendrix and now manages Slade.) "Paul was there with a bunch of friends at the table next to us and it was one of those things . . . just giving each other the eye, we just fancied each other," she later told the music paper *Sounds*. They started talking, and when the group decided to move on to another club, the Speakeasy, Linda was invited to go along with them. She found herself part of a crowd that included Eric Clapton, the late Brian Jones, Keith Moon, Pete Townshend and Roger Daltrey. They met again at a party to launch the "Sgt. Pepper" album; a special party for a few journalists and photographers that Brian Epstein held at his home in Chapel Street, Belgravia.

After that, they didn't see each other again for nearly a year—until Paul McCartney and John Lennon flew to New York to launch Apple in the United States with a press conference for American journalists, and appearances on US television. Linda went along to the conference, slipped into the front row with her camera in her hand, and McCartney said "Hi—how are you?" as she started taking photographs. As the press conference broke up, they started talking . . . and next day she drove out to Kennedy Airport with them as they prepared to fly back to London.

Although it was not known at the time, Paul soon flew back to New York to be with her; then they travelled down to California together—and then after he had returned to London he phoned her and asked: "Do you fancy coming to England?"

In that *Sounds* interview, Linda said that when she told her father about the phone call he said: "It's a pity you won't be able to go. You can't go, you have to take the child to school . . ." Then she added: "I thought: 'What do you mean, I won't be able to go?' Anyway, I came over and we lived together for a while, neither of us talked about marriage. We just loved each other and lived together, we liked each other a lot, so being conventional people one day I thought, okay let's get married—we love each other, let's make it definite. It was just like that, and that surprised so many people. Paul was a definite bachelor, he had every chick in town after him . . . he must have been crazy to get married. But, you know, we are happy, and happiness is the main thing."

Already, they had holidayed together on Paul's farm in Scotland; Heather had stayed over in London, forming a close and natural relationship with McCartney; and then suddenly they were married—on 11th March, 1969, Linda popped down to the Marylebone Register Office and gave twenty-four hours' notice of their intentions, and the next day—when all Fleet Street knew the news—they were married by Registrar Mr. E. R. Sanders, with Paul slipping on Linda's second finger a gold ring that he had rather hurriedly bought for £12 the night before.

To the outside world it seemed a hurried wedding; the night before he was in the recording studios working on a Jackie Lomax track "Thumbin' A Ride" (Lomax was one of the earliest Apple artists, and had formerly been in a Liverpool group The Undertakers that had worked on the same club and ballroom circuit as The Beatles in the very early days)—and on his wedding night Paul returned to the studios and finished off the track!

But hurried or not, it was a well-publicised wedding; photographers and journalists from the Fleet Street papers started gathering outside McCartney's home in Cavendish Avenue, St. John's Wood, from around 6 am on the morning of 12th March—which meant a wait of nearly four hours because Paul and Linda were not due to be married until 9:45 am, and even then there was another hour's delay after that because his brother Mike, who had been invited to be Best Man, was held up by a train breakdown travelling from Birmingham. Luckily for the McCartneys, there were no other weddings booked that day at St. Marylebone—so they were able to wait there until Mike arrived, running breathless up the stairs through the crowd of waiting pressmen to say: "Forgive me, it wasn't my fault. Have you been done?" To which Paul replied: "No—we've been waiting for you!"

Afterwards, Paul and Linda invited the journalists back to their home, offered round champagne, and answered the inevitable questions. How had they met? Paul referred back to that New York press conference and how she had always been at the back of his mind from the day he first saw her, adding "but we didn't get to know each other until we went out for a night on a bit of a thrash." Were they going on honeymoon? "No—not till later," said Paul. Where had they bought the ring? Paul admitted that he had forgotten all about it until after the shops closed—and had then knocked up a jeweller and bought one for £12. Was Linda part of the Eastman-Kodak family? No, she said—and Paul pulled a face and complained, "I've been done—where's the money?"

Later, when Paul started writing songs with Linda, forming their own band together, Wings, and when Paul began the High Court action against the other Beatles after they had recruited Allen Klein, the music papers became almost hysterically abusive against Linda. It was suggested that she had too great an influence over him, that it was because of her that the split with John, George and Ringo had developed, that she had little talent—but my own feeling always was that this was an unfair and unnecessarily hurtful attitude for them to take.

Indeed, having met them both for a long, private interview, and having seen them together on other occasions, having heard the music that Paul has written since she came into his life, and having spoken to a great many other people who have either worked with them or known them well, having seen them working together as Wings, handling press conferences, performing on stage, always behaving quite normally (though a little tenseness always does show through in these sort of events), I have believed for a long time now that her influence has never been anything but good.

The very fact that they have tried to live a quite normal life together has probably been the one factor that has made them more misunderstood; people don't expect it and the Press don't expect it, either. It's strange but after all the rock 'n' roll sensations and scandals of the Sixties few people expect stars like Paul McCartney to be normal any more, which is nonsensical because I have always found that nearly all the top artistes remain very ordinary people indeed in their everyday lives, that those who do not rarely survive, and the only deep change in personality develops in the attitudes of other people towards them, particularly in the press.

So far as the McCartneys are concerned, their life is very normal indeed, and their wealth has enabled them to keep it so. Since their marriage two daughters, Stella and Mary, have been born, and they live and travel as a family between their homes in London and Scotland, seeing a great deal of their grandparents, aunts, uncles and other relatives in Liverpool and New York. Apart from a daily housekeeper, Rose, Linda does all the work around the home herself, with the children encouraged to lend a hand, whether it be washing dishes or helping in the kitchen. "This is what I like to see," Linda told *Woman's Own*. "If parents have money and hire maids and nannies, children never learn to be independent and do things for themselves. People are always surprised at how good our kids are when we're travelling. If you travel together like us you have got to get a system. When we go through an airport it's 'Everybody hold hands, everybody be quiet!' If this doesn't work, well, I'm not at all the type to be embarrassed at smacking a kid in front of other people."

In fact, the amount of travelling they do is not so much as people often might think. When recording abroad, the whole family travels together, and at Christmas they always spend part of the holiday with grandparents either in Liverpool or New York, and in the other school holidays they are usually to be found at the farm in Scotland. Apart from that the McCartneys are mainly London-based, with their children going to school in the city. "Having the children travelling with us on shows means they are not too conscious of having a famous father. The fans, the shows—the children are part of it all the time, so it's just life to them. And we're just Mum and Dad," Linda said in that same *Woman's Own* interview. She added that Paul's own family life around Liverpool was not very different to her own background: "My family was very close. My father's parents—they're dead now—were Russian immigrants, very warm, down-to-earth working class people. My Dad just happened to be born intelligent and worked his way through Harvard Law School . . . I was a career woman before I met Paul, but I always had a base at home. I believe in equal pay and all that but I wouldn't want my husband to do the ironing."

Likewise, she told me that in London they would sometimes dine out or go to a show like "Godspell," "Jesus Christ, Superstar" or "Applause" and maybe go on to Tramps in Jermyn Street afterwards, but they would be just as likely to stay at home, with Linda cooking the evening meal, maybe a three-course meal if three or four friends were joining them for the evening—or if they were alone it might be just fish and chips. One thing she is strict about is that the food is never packaged from a tin or a refrigerator; in London their vegetables are bought fresh—and in Scotland they have their own vegetable garden growing potatoes, turnips, parsnips, spinach, broad and runner beans, sprouts, lettuce and salad stuffs . . . and a greenhouse to grow their own tomatoes. "We are mostly vegetarian, but we do eat meat occasionally, like eggs and bacon, sausages . . . or a slice of smoked salmon on scrambled eggs, which is a little dish we both like," she said.

Now, there is no-one else living in the house with them like there was before McCartney met Linda. Rose, the housekeeper, comes by day and is treated as almost part of the family ("She's like an auntie—I don't know where we'd be without her," says Linda)—and if they need a babysitter in the evening then their secretary at Paul's London office (he has a small suite of rooms in Soho with a

personal manager, an accountant and secretarial staff) or-
ganises one for them for the evening.

In Scotland, their life is much less sophisticated; they
get the groceries themselves from Campbeltown—and
Paul spends much of his day out on the farm. (For one
Christmas, Linda gave him a tractor as a present—and he
gave her twelve pheasants!) "We've got no cows," Paul told
me, emphasising that being hilly and rather bleak country
it was more suitable for rearing sheep, "but we've got
about 150 to 200 sheep, and every year I do the shearing
myself, using the hand shears . . . then we send off the
wool to the Wool Marketing Board. Linda has been wanting to use our own wool to make our own blankets, but so
far we haven't been able to get that organised."

The sheep are never killed, though occasionally some
are sent to market. "I couldn't bring myself to see them
being killed," Paul told me. "We just let them breed and
multiply, and every year we try to breed them, scientifi-
cally, so far as we can . . . we try to keep them down to
thirty lambs a year, by keeping the ewes behind a fence—
but that's unless one of the rams leaps over the fence. I
love the life we have up there, and the kids love it—
they're all animal mad." And having so much land, they
keep their own horses so that the whole family can go riding when they want to. There are six horses up there, including Drake's Drum, the racehorse that Paul once
bought as a birthday present for his father, which he once
led himself into the winners' enclosure at Aintree, and who
is now enjoying what Paul calls "an early retirement." The
other horses are Honor (Paul's); Cinnamon (Linda's) and
three ponies, Coconut, Cookie and Sugarfoot.

"We lead a very simple life up there," he said. "We get
up in the morning . . . I light the fire . . . Linda starts
the breakfast, and maybe Heather will do the washing-up,
and then I'll be working round the garden or on the farm
while Linda's cooking, or some days maybe we'll go out riding, and then sometimes we'll work on some songs in the
barn—it's just a barn because there's no-one living near
enough to us for it to need sound-proofing . . . and then

in the evenings after supper, we'll all sit down and watch TV. It's just a quite peaceful, quiet life, that's all it is."

Asked in that *Sounds* interview whether Paul was a good husband, Linda said: "Very much so, I don't think they come better. We both come from families where the parents loved each other very much and my mother and father, until my mother died, were married for twenty-five years . . . the same with Paul's parents—his mother is no longer alive—but they loved each other." Asked by *Disc and Music Echo* about his views on educating the children, Paul replied: "I don't like Mary going to school. I think she's too young . . . sometimes we keep her home, because I don't think five is all that brilliant an age to go to school. They are still very tiny at five, and school gets them grown up too quickly. I'm not fussy about education—Linda's not very well educated. She's educated, but I know a lot of people who aren't and they're still really great people. So I don't place very heavy emphasis on it; I know some people who are very well educated and are absolute bums. In a family I think you teach each other a lot simply by living together. We were going to teach Heather to read, but we thought we'd wait and see if she showed any interest in it. Then one day we got her a horse book and that was it. Now her nose is never out of books, especially horse books . . . it's a genuine love, instead of something rammed down her throat." To me Linda said of Heather's school: "She likes it because the school seems to give her what she needs, but they don't seem to learn much these days to my mind. I was never very good at school. I dreamt my way through it . . . and I was brought up fairly strictly in Scarsdale. You know how it is—they want you to come top in everything all the time. Fierce competition all the time. I'm quite the opposite in the way I bring up my kids. I leave Heather to herself pretty much—I'm not at all interested in breathing over her shoulder all the time. All the same, she's incredible. She reads and writes a lot, and is very artistic. She loves painting. She has very high morals, like at school she is the one who never misses feeding and cleaning out the rabbits, and putting down clean newspaper in their cages. Only the other day, she brought the newspaper to me, opened at a page of some naked ladies, and asked: 'Mummy, do you think it's good or bad that anyone—even children—can open a newspaper and see pictures of naked people?' Now, what do you make of that?"

This then, is the McCartneys' life today. They are totally happy, bound up in the lives of their children, relaxed, free of anxieties, natural, though privileged in the sense that they are able to afford to divide their time between homes in London and Scotland, families in Britain and America, and working holidays in Lagos, Jamaica, Nashville, or wherever a suitable studio and the right conditions might be available. For some people, that could be a crazy existence—but not for them. The McCartneys are wholly at ease, and out of it all is coming some really outstanding, tender, gentle and controlled rock 'n' roll music.

Chapter Seven

Over the years since they met and married, and particularly since Paul McCartney started recording with his own permanent group of musicians, Wings, and making occasional live appearances again, Linda has been the butt for many cruel jokes within the music business and in the music press. It has been suggested that it was she who was mostly responsible for the break-up of The Beatles; that she was the dominant personality in their marriage, and that because of her his talent as a songwriter went into a period of decline. These are theories that I have never been able to accept. It was not all that silly for McCartney to have wanted his in-laws to have handled The Beatles' legal affairs at one stage—because they do happen to be amongst the world's leading show business lawyers, and the argument that he is under Linda's thumb is just not credible to anyone who knows just how tough each of The Beatles has had to be over the years, and how basically conventional they both are in their views on marriage. And as for those attempts to analyse McCartney's music and to relate his songs to different periods in his life, suggesting that there was one style of music from 1962-66, and then another from 1966-70, with a quite different phase in more recent years as his work with Wings has become more accomplished with the "Red Rose Speedway" and "Band On The Run" albums and such exceptional individual tracks as "My Love," "Jet" and "Maybe I'm Amazed"— well, I find that theory almost incomprehensible, and an attempt at over-sophistication on the part of the theorists.

Personally, I believe there has been no great change in McCartney's style at any point in his carreer; love songs and relationships between people have always been the basis of his work, but equally he's been capable of turning his hand to rock "n" roll with the best of them, and has been subject to just as many influences as Lennon or any other contemporary writer; a McCartney song is a McCartney song, whether written in his teens, in his early days with The Beatles, or more recently. His stamp is unmistakeable—it's just that as the years have gone by his knowledge of recording techniques has improved, his experience has widened, and he's got better at it. When he has the time to work on a project the result has been better than when he's been working to too tight a schedule (people forget that the very first Beatles album comprised songs they had been playing for years, and was recorded in twelve hours flat—and it wasn't until three or four years later when their recording schedule became more relaxed that they were able to find that extra time to produce work like "Sgt. Pepper," on which they spent 700 hours in the recording studios). The only time he has approached anything that could be in any way described as a duff album was when The Beatles were in a state of turmoil, and he brought out the "McCartney" LP, playing every instrument himself, and overdubbing all the tracks—and even that was an album that most musicians would be proud of.

The one thing that can be truly noted is that while he was locked in dispute with the other Beatles, and pondering whether or not to commence legal proceedings to protect what he saw as his interests, his work suffered (which is not so very surprising); and once the personal problems had been resolved, the Receiver had been appointed, and the others had come round to the view that he could have been right all along, his work improved again (and that's not so surprising, either).

Another factor that is interesting about McCartney's work is that he keeps developing musical ideas that he has had for years—even on that "McCartney" album there was one track, "Hot As Sun," that he had first written back in 1958 and had never recorded before, and there was another track, "Junk," that he had first worked on out in India when he and others were studying transcendental meditation with the Maharishi. This disproves almost completely the "periods-theory" about his work, for in reality he still has dozens of ideas to be worked on, songs that have been half-finished, maybe just a few bars of melody or a riff.

His first songs were written long before he, Lennon and Harrison formed The Beatles. As early as the late Fifties while he was still attending Liverpool Institute and while the three of them were already playing together as The Quarrymen, those first numbers were taking shape. By their first No. 1 single in 1963, and the formation of their song publishing company, he and John Lennon between them had over a hundred songs that they had written together—at least that was their claim, because in those early years all their songs were said to have been written jointly, whereas in fact quite frequently The Beatles would record numbers that had been wholly written by either Lennon or McCartney.

The first song McCartney ever wrote was titled "I Lost My Little Girl," which has still not been recorded (the theme was wholly imaginary; talking about that song in an interview with the now-defunct magazine *Rave* he said he hadn't lost his girlfriend at all!) In an early interview with the *New Musical Express*, he recalled some other songs he had written around the same time: "I was lucky enough to get ten bob a week pocket money—but it didn't go far. If I was taking a girl to the pictures I had to work it out exactly—3d for the bus from my house to the pictures, 2s 6d each to go in, and about 2s for ices or nuts and a packet of ciggies. I used to walk home if I didn't have enough left for the fare. But I never minded that. I wrote lots of songs on those walks home—'World Without Love' and 'Love of the Loved' included . . ." Other nights he would walk home from John Lennon's house in Menlove Avenue, where they often used to play guitar in the bathroom, where the acoustics were thought to be rather better, and on those walks he said: "I had to cross this horrible pitch black golf course. Anyway, I'd always be singing, but if ever I came across somebody in the dark, I'd shut up and try to pretend it hadn't been me. Met a copper like that once. I had a guitar around my neck and was quite cheerfully playing and singing at the top of my voice as I walked. Thought he was going to arrest me. But he walked up and asked if I'd give him guitar lessons." Of the two songs he referred to, "World Without Love" was a No. 1 hit for Peter and Gordon and "Love of the Loved" was Cilla Black's first single, but in both cases it was subsequently said that they were joint Lennon and McCartney compositions.

This is something that is often misunderstood about their writing—the occasions when they actually sat down together, working like painters with a blank canvas, were comparatively rare. Usually, either Lennon or McCartney would have the idea for a lyric or a melody first, and often have it nearly completed, and then the other would suggest a change of emphasis, altering the middle eight or perhaps tightening up a lyric—but just as often they would finish their own songs themselves, and you could usually tell who had written which by listening to their recordings together and seeing who handled the lead vocal.

When writing together their approach to songwriting was never as devotedly intellectual, political or subliminal as the hordes of phoney musicologists have since tried to suggest. It is nothing less than sheer bunkum to imply that "Lucy In The Sky with Diamonds" was all about the drug LSD (in fact the title was a phrase that Lennon picked up in childhood conversation with his son Julian). Likewise the reference to Henry the Horse in "Being for the Benefit of Mr. Kite" had nothing whatsoever to do with heroin. The whole idea for that song came from a Victorian circus poster that Lennon used to have framed on the wall of his home in Weybridge—and if you ever happen to see another copy of the poster in a print shop you will see that Pablo Fanque's Circus Royal was actually presented at the Town Meadows, Rochdale, in February, 1843. It is also nonsense to say that "A Day In The Life" was also drug-inspired. That number as it happens was two earlier songs coupled together—with part of it inspired by a story Len-

Paul McCartney 1974

2 a John

b Paul

c George

d Ringo

(top) Paul and Linda at Ossie Clark's fashion show 1974
(bottom) Paul and Linda back-stage after their concert at the City
Hall, Newcastle 1973

4 (top) Paul and Linda with other members of Wings, on top of their bus
converted and hired for a two month tour of Europe, 1972
(bottom) Paul plays host on the Christmas edition of BBC-TV's
The Wonderful World of Disney

5 Wings 1974

6 (top) Paul, Linda and Wings with their converted bus
(bottom) Superfan Ken Krinsky catches the ear of his idol. Their
meeting in Manchester was arranged by Paul's tour manager

7 Denny Laine

8 (top) Wings afloat
 (bottom) Linda and Denny

9 Linda McCartney at their London office in Soho 1973

10 (top) Denny Laine at Oxford New Theatre 1973
    (bottom) Paul and Linda with Stella, their youngest daughter

11 Paul and Linda 1974

12 Paul McCartney's Wings with recent Gold Discs

13 (top) Wings at Top of the Pops
(bottom) Paul and Linda McCartney with family at London Airport

14 Paul McCartney pictured with brother Mike McGear whose latest album he has just produced

16 Wings 1974

non had read in the *Daily Mail*. McCartney's songs throughout—both when he and Lennon were popularly believed to be always writing together and more recently when he has either been writing on his own or with Linda—have tended to be love songs, whereas Lennon more frequently turns to other subjects.

"It's always been sort of traditional to have love as a theme for songs . . . it's a nice subject," McCartney once told *Disc and Music Echo*, and it's clearly a feeling that he still retains, for even now many of his better songs are romantic and based on ideas, memories and images that date back even to childhood. It is not something that I am going to attempt to analyse because it has always been my belief that this type of musicology is at best bizarre and pretentious and at worst untruthful—it is no more worthwhile to analyse the magic of a song than it is to dissect the colours of a butterfly or the flight of a swallow. Each has a quality of its own that is beyond analysis. But I have always been fascinated, as I believe most people are, by the way that songs are born—how the ideas develop, who gets them, and what happens from there. From my own interviews, it is possible to piece together some of the *history* of Lennon and McCartney's music (though with over two hundred songs published and with each of them now individually prolific, this is really a large enough subject for a book of its own).

Thus one can say that "From Me To You," which was their second No. 1 hit in Britain, was written on February 28th, 1963, while they were making their first British tour with Helen Shapiro, and were travelling by coach from York to Shrewsbury, where they were due to appear at the Granada cinema. McCartney and Lennon had been reading the *New Musical Express*, whose weekly readers' letters column used to be titled "From You To Us"—and from bending that phrase the idea developed. John Lennon told the same paper some time later: "We'd already written 'Thank You Girl' as the follow-up to 'Please Please Me'. This new number was to be the B-side. Anyway, there were we, not taking ourselves seriously. Just fooling about on the guitar. This went on for a while. Then we began to get a good melody line and we really started to work at it. Before that journey was over, we'd completed the lyric, everything. We were so pleased we knew we just had to make it the A-side."

Film producer Walter Shenson told me how another of their songs was born, the title song for their first film, "A Hard Day's Night": "Our schedule was two thirds through, and we still hadn't got a title. Then one day I was having lunch with The Beatles in the studio canteen. Much to his embarrassment, the other three were telling me the funny things Ringo did with the English language. A few nights before, John told me, they had all arrived back late after a hectic recording session. John said what a hard day it had been. Ringo pointed to the clock. 'You mean a hard day's night, don't you?' he said. As John was speaking, we all put down our knives and forks and looked at one another. 'That's it,' snapped Paul. At that moment we all knew we had found our film title. Straight after lunch, I cabled New York for approval. United Artists replied within the hour; they were delighted."

That night, driving home with them in their chauffeur-driven Austin Princess, Shenson mentioned how nice it would be to have a title song. "But you haven't a scene left to take one," said Lennon. "I could put it over the credits," said Shenson.

Lennon slumped back in his seat, and was silent for a few minutes. Then he leaned forward to chauffeur Bill Corbett. "Drive faster," said Lennon. "I'm inspired . . ." Next morning, he arrived at the studio at eight o'clock, and slapped a piece of paper down on Shenson's desk, picked up his guitar and said: "I'll show you how it goes." After a few bars, McCartney joined in, fitting in something like the harmony—and that evening the song was recorded.

Many of the songs that Lennon and McCartney wrote together were born just as casually as this—"Rocky Raccoon" was another number that they wrote relaxing between sessions with the Maharishi out in India; "Birthday" was one that Paul and John wrote together at Paul's home in St. John's Wood after they had cut short a recording session so that they could watch the rock 'n' roll film "The Girl Can't Help It" on TV; "Hold Me Tight" was a song they wrote years before they started recording and was a number they used to play at the Cavern; "Paperback Writer" was a song that Paul wrote largely because the word "paperback" was one that appealed to him; "Eleanor Rigby" was a song that Paul wrote at home.

"We put all our imagination and ideas into our songs," he told the *New Musical Express*. "They take so much concentration. 'Paperback Writer'? Well, this came about because I love the word 'paperback' . . . when we did the song, we wrote the words down like we were writing a letter . . . we sort of started off 'Dear Sir or Madam,' then carried on from there. If you look at the words, I think you'll see what I mean, the way they flow like a letter. But that's it, really, there's no story behind it . . ."

He explained how "Eleanor Rigby" came about in an interview with *The Sunday Times*: "I was sitting at the piano when I thought of it. Just like Jimmy Durante. The first few bars just came to me. And I got this name in my head—Daisy Hawkins, picks up the rice in the church where a wedding has been. I don't know why. I can hear a whole song in one chord. In fact, I think you can hear a whole song in one note, if you listen hard enough. But nobody ever listens hard enough . . . I couldn't think of much more, so I put it away for a day. Then the name Father McCartney came to me—and all the lonely people. But I thought people would think it was supposed to be my Dad, sitting knitting his socks. Dad's a happy lad. So I went through the telephone book and I got the name McKenzie. I was in Bristol when I decided Daisy Hawkins wasn't a good name. I walked round looking at the shops and I saw the name Rigby . . . then I took it down to John's house in Weybridge. We sat around laughing, got stoned and finished it off . . . all of our songs come out of our imagination. There never was an Eleanor Rigby."

Among the songs that Lennon has acknowledged as being mainly written by Paul McCartney—in a very detailed interview with *Record Mirror*, published in October, 1971—are "Love Me Do," most of which he said Paul wrote when he was about sixteen; "P.S. I Love You"; "I'll Be On My Way"; "All My Loving"; "I Wanna Be Your Man", a number that The Rolling Stones also recorded and which Lennon said was mostly written by McCartney, though he helped him finish it off; "I'll Keep You Satisfied," which was recorded by Billy J. Kramer; "Can't Buy Me Love"; "Like Dreamers Do"; "One and One Is Two"; "I'll Follow The Sun"; "She's A Woman", which Lennon also contributed to; "Yesterday," which was wholly Paul's composition and which he recorded with a string quartet; "Paperback Writer"; "Love of the Loved"; "Here, There and Everywhere"; "For No-one"; "Got To Get You Into My Life," a song that Paul also produced for Cliff Bennett and The Rebel Rousers and one on which Lennon said he thought George Harrison also helped; "Penny Lane," on which Lennon helped with the lyric; "A Little Help From My Friends"; "Getting Better"; "When I'm Sixty Four," though John helped with some of the lines; "Back in the USSR"; and "Why Don't We Do It In The Road," which Lennon said he thought was one of McCartney's best songs.

Among the songs that Lennon said were directly attributable to McCartney were "I Saw Her Standing There"; "Tip Of My Tongue"; "Nobody I Know"; "Things We Said Today"; "Don't Want To See You Again"; "I'm Down"; "The Night Before"; "Another Girl"; "Tell Me What You See"; "I've Just Seen A Face"; "That Means A Lot"; "You Won't See Me"; "I'm Looking Through You"; "Woman"; "Sgt. Pepper's Lonely Hearts Club Band"; "Fixing A Hole"; "Lovely Rita"; "Hello Goodbye"; "Your Mother Should Know"; "Fool On The Hill"; "Step Inside Love", which was another of Cilla Black's hits, and used by her as the theme song for a TV series; "Ob La Di, Oba La Da"; "Martha My Dear," which was a song inspired by Paul's sheepdog Martha; "Blackbird"; "I Will"; "Mother Nature's Son"; "Helter Skelter"; "Honey Pie," which Paul was to later say was suggested by the Twenties-style songs his father used to like; "Lady Madonna"; "All Together Now"; "Get Back"; "Let It Be"; "Maxwell's Silver Hammer"; "Oh Darling"; "You Never Give Me Your Money"; "She Came In Through the Bathroom Window"; "Golden Slumbers"; "Carry That Weight"; "Two of Us" and "The Long and Winding Road".

Perhaps the most fascinating thing about this list is that it gives the lie to the widespread belief that it was Lennon who wrote the rock numbers and McCartney who penned the ballads—for amongst these songs are the whole range of The Beatles' music, solid rock numbers like "Get Back," "Lady Madonna" or "I'm Down"; softly melodic songs like "Blackbird" or "Fool On The Hill"; songs with a story like "When I'm Sixty Four"; the almost Hendrix-style "Helter Skelter"; the rhythm 'n' blues-based "I Wanna Be Your Man," and the sentimental songs like "Penny Lane" (which was all about their memories of Liverpool), "Martha My Dear" or "The Long and Winding Road."

In one very revealing quote, talking on yet another occasion to the *New Musical Express,* whose coverage of The Beatles in the Sixties was exceptionally thorough, Paul McCartney said: "We are family grocers. You want yoghurt, we give you it. You want cornflakes, we have that too. Mums and Dads can't take some of our album stuff, so we make it simple for them on singles . . ." And in another interview with the same paper, he said: "I never usually write a song and think, 'Right, now this is going to be about something specific.' It's just that the words happen. I never try to make any serious social point. Just words to go with the music—and you can read anything you like into it . . . the way the words just come into your head is like John writing his books . . . I don't know how he does it, and he doesn't know how he does it. But he just writes and people who do create and write do it like that. It just flows into their heads and then into their hands . . ."

But I suspect the one part of his relationship with Lennon that he missed when The Beatles started feuding was having someone who would listen to the latest song he had written, and offer constructive advice; after all, that was really the nub of their work together—the way they would each give a second opinion to the other when it was needed. And this quite clearly is where Linda is now so important to him musically. Even before they met, music had been important to her; when The Beatles recorded "Let It Be" she joined in on the backing vocals, and when he recorded the whole of the "McCartney" solo album although he played every instrument, and recorded it at home (as you can hear from doors shutting and children chattering in the background), and Linda was there with him throughout.

"It was Paul who originally said he would teach me to play," she told me. "I'd said I wanted to play, but how could I? I had muffed all those lessons as a child. Paul told me that everyone has to start somewhere, and that when he started he didn't know anything, either . . . so I've learnt to play . . . at first I was terribly nervous of playing on stage in case I let the others down, but you know it was really great once those initial nerves were over. Now, I really enjoy myself when I'm playing . . . everyone else in the band has had years of experience, and I'm very inexperienced. But I'm learning all the time . . ." and to *Sounds,* she said: "He asked me to be in the band. After The Beatles broke up he had no friends he really wanted to work with, so he did the 'McCartney' album on his own and played everything, but I sang harmonies with him. Now I'm into Moog and on 'Band On the Run' I play a lot of the Moog parts. I also like to play Mellotron, and piano . . ."

As this started to work, his music improved; this is no abstract theory—just listen to "McCartney" and then "Ram" and then "Wings Wild Life" and you can hear the style developing and then progressing, until by the time you reach the "Red Rose Speedway" and "Band On The Run" albums the melodies and the rock numbers are as tightly controlled and as disciplined as ever they were in his work with The Beatles. That is not to say they are better, because you can never compare songs any more than you can analyse them. But they do stand on their own and

102

numbers like "One More Kiss," "My Love," "Little Lamb Dragonfly," "Jet" and "Let Me Roll It" are very fine songs indeed. They are the work of a man who has found himself.

Chapter Eight

When Paul McCartney first broke with The Beatles, he worked almost wholly on his own, with some help from Linda who had until then never worked as a musician. They quickly organised themselves, setting up their own office in Soho—employing a manager, an accountant, sometimes a publicist, and a succession of secretaries. But despite his wealth, the offices were very unpretentious—when I went there to interview one of his secretaries, Rebecca Hinds, I quickly noticed there was lino on the floor, not carpets; that the desks were second hand, and so was the filing cabinet, which had clearly known better days.

"It's an everyday working office," Rebecca told me, explaining that she began work there every morning between 9:30 am and 10 am, sometimes calling round at the McCartneys' house during the day, and quite often working on until late in the evening because it was not until then that phone calls started to come through from the Eastmans' office in New York.

She explained that she had been sharing a flat with some girls who worked as secretaries in the music business, and through them heard that Shelley Turner, who was then running the McCartneys' office for them, was herself looking for a secretary. "She's really a writer, and she's now gone back to writing," said Rebecca, who phoned her up, and was asked whether she would like to spend a day at the office to see if they both worked well together.

"One Thursday I was due to have the day off from my other job, so I spent the day here, helping in the office, and Shelley and I found that we got on well, and it was then that she suggested that I have an interview with Paul and Linda, who were then getting their group together. I was a bit nervous about that, and did not know what to expect, but they were very nice to me, asked me what organising experience I had, and whether I thought I could organise things for a group—they were much more concerned about whether I could organise than about my typing and shorthand, though I had both those. So I told them that if I could organise six architects, which had been my job before, I was quite sure I could organise their office—and they gave me the job."

That was in 1971, after Paul had already produced his first solo album, on which he played every instrument himself which was not difficult since he played bass, rhythm and lead guitar; was accomplished at piano and organ; could play some brass instruments if he had to—and was a better drummer than most people knew. (Even when The Beatles were out in Hamburg, he had once supplemented a week's money by sitting in with Tony Sheridan's band on drums for a week—and had often been known to sit in with different groups on drums.)

Nevertheless, this was no substitute for actually working with a group of musicians, which was what McCartney most wanted to do. For some time after The Beatles had stopped touring he had tried to persuade the others to start making concert appearances again, and had even suggested at one stage that they appear anonymously at small clubs, so anxious was he to have the stimulus of working before a live audience. So he had had this idea at the back of his mind that he would recruit his own group of musicians for recording purposes, and that if it worked he would make the line-up a permanent one.

It was he who suggested that Linda should start playing, too, if she wanted to—and when she hesitated and said that she had not played an instrument since childhood, McCartney said there was no reason why she should not start again if she wished. Inevitably, when they started appearing together—the world famous bass guitarist, who had won numerous awards, playing with his wife—he was ridiculed by other musicians and by the music press. He admitted later that perhaps the idea would have been more acceptable from the start had he announced it in advance by going on one of the TV chat shows, saying he was anxious to play in a live group again just for the fun of it, and that Linda was starting to play from scratch. As it was, nearly everything they did was judged by absurdly critical standards—despite the fact one of the first songs they wrote together, "Another Day," was a Number One hit in this country, and sold over a million copies world-wide, and the first album they worked on together, "Ram," was noticeably better than the "McCartney" album.

To make that second album, they had flown to the States intending to hire a session drummer in New York—and that was how they met Denny Seiwell. Seiwell whose father had also been a professional drummer, had been brought up in Pennsylvania, moved to New York, where he had worked on jazz and soul sessions, and appeared frequently at the Half Note Club with visiting jazz stars like Zoot Sims, though outside the music business itself he was not a particularly well known drummer—and was but one of nine American drummers that McCartney had arranged to meet and audition in a New York cellar club. When Seiwell arrived there, he found himself faced with the worst possible equipment because this was the way McCartney thought he would test them all to see who coped with the situation best.

I subsequently asked McCartney what it was about Seiwell that distinguished him from the others, and he replied: "Well, actually it was his tom toms. That may not sound much to anyone who is not a musician . . . but if you see a drummer playing tom toms, you learn a lot about him."

McCartney was pleased with the sessions that produced the "Ram" LP, and after they had finished he asked Seiwell if he would like to become a permanent member of the group he was planning to form—though at that stage McCartney had no other musicians in mind, and no name for the group. Seiwell agreed, and moved to Scotland himself with his wife, Monique, settling on a farm near

106

McCartney's home, where he liked to practise in one of the barns, and record in a studio that he had fitted out himself nearby.

The next musician that McCartney approached was someone whom he had admired for some years, and whose name he had frequently mentioned in interviews—Denny Laine, whom he had known socially five years earlier when Denny was a member of the Moody Blues. I asked McCartney what made him approach Laine, and he replied: "I don't know, really. It's one of those things when you're starting a band . . . several ideas go through your head, different names are suggested to you, and then I remembered 'Go Now.' That was the single Denny made with the Moody Blues, and it has always been one of my favourite records . . ."

But in the five or six years until McCartney formed Wings in 1971, he had neither seen nor spoken to Denny Laine, though they had seen quite a lot of each other in the early Sixties. By 1971, Denny was thinking of recording a solo album of his own songs after being in several abortive groups, and was living in one room at the back of his manager Tony Secunda's Mayfair office, and it was there that he received McCartney's phone call offering him the job with the band. Denny had been fast asleep on a mattress on the floor. "Hello, Denny. This is Paul. I'm thinking of forming a band to go out on the road—are you interested?" asked McCartney.

I was the first person to talk to Denny about the invitation, and he told me at the time that he did not find it surprising, which I found hard to believe. "You see, we're friends," he said. "We know each other. We know how the other feels, and what the other does."

Since leaving the Moody Blues, Denny had spent years searching for musical satisfaction—he has never been a very materialistic person, and even now lives on a houseboat on the Thames because, he once explained to me, he has a "horror of being in debt, and getting involved in things like mortgages."

After the Moody Blues, he ran his own string band; made solo records; spent two years planning what turned

107

out to be a very short-lived group indeed, Balls—and in between all this had lived in Spain. There, he spent a year living with gypsies in Andalucia, learning flamenco guitar. "I've always liked the basic music of a country," he told me. "I like their folk songs. To me, pub songs are folk songs—and flamenco is the folk music of Spain. I was able to live very cheaply out there, on just twelve shillings a day, which included my rent for a little artist's shed next to a pig sty, which I shared with an American, Charles Jackson. He came from a wealthy family, and told me he was descended from General Jackson, but he was running away from the Draft, and he wanted to learn flamenco, too.

"I always go where the musicians are. That's me. I've always liked to feel part of a community of musicians. Those gypsies in Andalucia are real musicians, but it's as hard for them to escape from there as it was for me to get away from Birmingham . . ."

Denny returned to London in 1969, meeting up with another musician who had come down from Birmingham with the mid-Sixties groups, Trevor Burton (who had been with The Move). Together with the drummer Alan White—who later worked with John Lennon on his Plastic Ono Band sessions and who is now with Yes—they lived in a cottage in Hampshire, rehearsing, writing, occasionally playing with other friends on sessions. At one stage, Denny and Trevor were invited to tour with Eric Clapton and Ginger Baker in Airforce.

By early 1971, Denny thought that he had enough of his own songs for a solo album, and was planning this at the flat the day that McCartney phoned him. "Paul told me that I'd get a call in a few days' time, and then I'd meet him up in Scotland at his farm," said Denny. As we talked then, I glanced around his one-roomed flat with its kitchen and bathroom off. On the walls were Victorian paintings, some religious in theme; in a glass display cabinet he had books on art, poetry and music; on the floor lay a pallette of paints—and beside it spread out on pages from *The Times* lay the pieces of an old marble clock that Denny had been cleaning and repairing when I arrived. A Bob Dylan album played in stereo in the background.

"I got the call," said Denny, "and then went up to Scotland, not having seen him up to that point, and staying over a couple of days in Birmingham on the way to see my family . . . Denny (Seiwell) met me at Glasgow airport, and then we caught a plane to Campbeltown, which is the nearest airport to Paul's home. We don't go that route now; Paul has an arrangement with a hire firm to travel by private jet whenever we need to, and we can fly direct from London to Campbeltown in little more than half an hour.

"Denny took me over to his house, and that night drove me over to Paul's farm, where we sat around, talking and drinking, discussing ideas for the band, and recalling the old days when we'd both been in groups that had come down to London from the provinces. Back in those days, musicians like The Beatles and the Moody Blues all used to go down to the clubs in the evenings not to rave it up, but to relax; that was all there was to it—the business wasn't frenetic like it is now. We all used to know each other, would call round at each other's homes when we weren't working, would meet up on tours and on TV shows, all working together in the same business, so Paul and I had a lot to talk about. I had been travelling that day for sixteen or seventeen hours, so I just fell asleep, and Paul and Denny carried me off to bed, tucked me up, and gave me a goodnight kiss. I'd been shattered by the journey . . ."

Over the next days and weeks, the four of them—the two Dennies, Paul and Linda—settled down to work, rehearsing in the barn adjoining the farmhouse, and then some days when the sun was shining they would go outside, rehearse in the open air, perched on the hillside with the sea (the Mull of Kintyre) all around them. "It's just a normal farm up there," Denny told me. "When Paul gets up in the mornings, and goes out on his tractor he works around the farm, growing vegetables, while Linda works around the house. When he is up there, Paul is just a farmer who plays guitar—he is not a Beatle any more.

"He lives off the land, grows all his own food. It's all

109

very simple. Every day the food is fresh, which food should be—and Linda is a real woman. She is busy in the house and she's a good cook, and looks after their children . . ."

Initially Paul was thinking that the group—which he eventually decided to call Wings—would be a four-member group; but this he found restrictive so he decided to bring in someone else to play lead guitar—which was how Henry McCullough, a long standing friend of Denny Laine's, came to join the group.

Although a much less outward-going personality, tending to be rather taciturn, Henry McCullough already had a considerable reputation as a guitarist through his work with The Grease Band, who regularly backed Joe Cocker. Like Rory Gallagher, Henry had started with the Irish show bands, which are quite different to anything that has ever been popular in Britain, and then eventually he came to England with Eire Apparent, a group that worked with Jimi Hendrix at one stage, sharing the same manager in Chas Chandler. In a profile of McCullough, *Melody Maker* once commented that he was "the eternal drifter, wandering from gig to gig, following his nose with his guitar to pay the rent. The future's never too clear when you talk to Henry, and his past is a blurred trail of events . . . around Dublin he's almost a legend now as the stories of his early days with the Skyrocket Showband have grown out of proportion. He was the longhaired looner playing with a bunch of straight musicians. After the Skyrockets, Henry played for a while with an Irish rock band with a black South African singer, Jean and the Gents, then Eire Apparent came along. Like so many Irish musicians and bands before them, they made their way to Blackpool and were managing to exist on six pounds a night before Chas Chandler discovered them at the UFO Club . . ." Henry had later worked with Sweeney's Men before teaming up with Joe Cocker, but the Grease Band had folded by the time McCartney asked him if he would like to join Wings.

"In fact it was Paul's roadie who rang, saying do you fancy sitting in," Henry told the *New Musical Express*. "After the Grease Band I didn't know what the hell was going on so I went down and had a play. That was Tuesday and afterwards things were left at that—nothing was said. Then I had another call on Thursday to go down again and afterwards Paul said, "Do you want to join our group?" Although I knew Denny Laine, I'd never met McCartney before. Once I got used to seeing him there in person, he turned out to be a great bloke. I guess I was a bit nervous but I had a couple of pints of Guinness before I went along the first time. That helped . . . McCartney wants to play everything. Surely that's the point of music—to have enough different material to play to audiences of twelve-year-olds or old age pensioners. Paul just wants to play the whole lot— heavy numbers, rock numbers, everything."

In fact, this was an outlook that all five members of Wings shared—though it rapidly became very misunderstood, especially with Linda McCartney also playing with them on piano and organ.

The first single they released together after Henry had completed the line-up was "Give Ireland Back to the Irish," which personally I did not like at all musically—but it was a simple song with a simple message and it said what McCartney, who had strong pro-Irish feelings, wanted to say at the time. (It was banned by the BBC because of its political content.) The second single they released was received with almost hysterical abuse in the music press and by McCartney's fellow musicians—though he saw nothing wrong (and neither do I) in releasing an up-dated nursery rhyme specially for very young children. But the music critics did not see it that way; they judged that single by the same standard that they had judged his work with The Beatles—which was as futile as criticising Lewis Carroll for writing "Alice in Wonderland" and not sticking to his true role as a teacher of mathematics. By the time their third single "Hi, Hi, Hi"/"C Moon" was released, the critics were in no mood to listen to McCartney's work dispassionately—though in fact that first number had been a show-stopper throughout Wings' first stage tour in Europe in the summer of 1972, and both numbers were as good as much of the work McCartney had done with The Beatles.

By the time the last two singles had been released, McCartney had already overcome the difficult psychological problem of appearing live again before audiences who had come to regard The Beatles as almost mythical demi-Gods; he did it by making his first appearances unannounced and unexpected until a few hours before each show at different British universities, and described afterwards in a press release what they had been trying to do:

"Performing hasn't changed any since I last went out. It's just a different band and different material. It could never change. Performing is performing. It's still just you singing a song . . . I hope as our little bit of the music scene grows and matures into something more steady it can bring with it an environment like the one in the past with music hall and theatrical people, allowing for that sort of interplay so that people could guest at each other's concerts or so that we could talk to Pete Townshend or whoever in the natural run of things without having to throw a party. I believe in the possibility within the framework of the music scene, although it's all sort of isolated now, because this kind of music will live forever."

Paul McCartney, Spring 1972

For Paul McCartney, it's people who matter. Whether it's the people who'd packed out The Cavern and sweated and sang and danced and cheered back in the early days . . . the people who'd followed The Beatles, who'd loved them and cried for them and grown with them as The Beatles grew . . . the people who still clung to every word he sang and every note he played . . . the people who shared with him, from whatever distance, his hopes and fears and happiness . . . the people—and this was around the turn of 1972—he hadn't seen or played to for six long years.

So it was, in February 1974 that Paul McCartney set off from outside his home in St. John's Wood to head for wherever fate—and music—were to take him. With him, in a rented caravan and a loaded Avis truck, went his wife Linda, their three children, three musicians—one with his wife—three dogs and a couple of roadies. Paul McCartney and Wings were on the road, and Paul—after six years—was to play again to the people who mattered.

They went unannounced and uninvited, headed to wherever they felt like going, and wherever there might be people who'd lend an ear. For all of them—for Paul and Linda, for Denny Laine, Henry McCullough and Denny Seiwell—it was a new beginning; the start of something so potentially big that it was almost frightening, and yet at the same time the start of something so natural and spontaneous that it seemed a little bit ridiculous, in retrospect, to think that it could possibly have happened in any other way. They went with no contracts, and no hassles . . . just the simple questions "Can we play here?" and "Where can we set up?" It had been Paul's dream, but it was one that all of them could share: to play, to entertain, and to have themselves a good time with anyone who felt like joining them.

Nottingham was their first step, for no other reason than it was the first place they came to. "We went into Nottingham University students' union at about five o'clock and fixed it up for lunchtime the next day," says Trevor, one of Wings' roadies. "Nottingham was the best because they were so enthusiastic. No hassles. No-one quite expected or believed it. Ian and I went down there at half-past eight the next morning with the gear. We threw a few posters up and put the word out on the tannoy."

Paul:	We never asked to be announced. We either strolled on stage or were, in fact, discovered playing.
Linda:	None of us took it too worriedly; we just arrived.
Denny L:	I wasn't nervous at Nottingham because we'd already gone through that one mentally, talking about it. By the time we actually came on it was easy.

Henry: I was nervous at first because of the way it was being done and because it was Wings . . . I was just hoping everything would go all right. Luckily it did.

Paul: It could have been a real panic.

From Nottingham they went to York, to Hull and then to Newcastle, to Lancaster, to Leeds and Sheffield . . . then Manchester, Birmingham and finally Swansea. Two weeks on the road, playing and talking music all the way:

Trevor: Paul was the only one who never seemed to get tired.

Henry: I felt he loved every minute of it—just getting back on the road and playing. In Manchester a policewoman looked in the back of the van and said, "Oh God!" People just couldn't believe it.

Denny L: To get good you have to be on the road, to have the audience pull you to pieces and put you back together again. Then you come into the studio and it's like a gig.

Henry: Being on the road is what it's all about. Like a circus. In my head, I'm on the road every day of the year. I couldn't live just doing studio work. I don't think anyone could. I think Paul finally realised that's what he missed. And it's what keeps a band really tight . . . It's the only way I think we could have done it . . . sneaking out like that. You have to work those places before you can take on Madison Square Gardens.

Denny L: If you are with the right people, it happens right because you enjoy it. You don't have to let people know where they stand all the time because they *know*. They're secure. There was a good mood. People were just happy to see Paul on the road again.

Paul: We went on tour knowing it would either bring us together, or we wouldn't be able to stand each other—which was something we had to find out. We got on remarkably, wanting to do a common thing . . .

So it was that Paul McCartney and Wings made their first vital step . . . to see that they could do it, and to see that they *wanted* to do it. Paul again: "Publicity alone can never do it. The nitty-gritty is the performer clicking. That only happens when the performer has direct contact with his audience. That's what life's all about, really . . . people, and the ability to reach them in a positive way. You either click with people or you don't. The degree depends on the intention."

Thus, in that press release, McCartney described clearly how he saw Wings. The important thing to him, as it has been for the past few years when the other Beatles had been reluctant to return to live concerts, had been to do just that and enjoy the atmosphere of an audience responding to his work. This is something that people outside music probably find hard to understand—but McCartney later told me, after he and Wings had made a much longer tour that summer of 1972 throughout Europe over a period of seven weeks, that the concert he had enjoyed most was one in which the audience was very cold to begin with, and which they really had to work hard to entertain, and which gradually warmed to the group, and then became very emotionally involved in their music. "That's what being a musician is all about," he told me.

With that first Wings line-up, McCartney undoubtedly had high ambitions; he launched the new band with a party at the Empire Ballroom, Leicester Square, to which the 1,000-odd guests were all invited to dress conventionally for an evening of Mecca ballroom fun. Among those that did were Elton John, Jimmy Page of Led Zeppelin, Keith Moon and John Entwistle of The Who, Deep Purple, Sandy Denny, Mary Hopkin, Terence Stamp, Gilbert O'Sullivan, The Faces, Mungo Jerry, Tony Blackburn, Pete Murray and Sandie Shaw. They danced to Ray McVay's band, watched a display of formation dancing—and bought their own drinks at the bar. With this ingenious piece of promotion, the music business realised that Wings had arrived.

Then they followed this with the release of the first two Wings' singles; with that low-key (but not unpublicised) tour of British universities, and then the summer McCartney and Wings began that European tour, which was also described as a happy jaunt. McCartney and the band travelled from country to country (the schedule is given in the appendix) in a highly decorated London bus, and the only sour note was struck when Customs Officials in Denmark discovered that cannabis was being posted to them from London (see appendix). Their secretary Rebecca Hinds travelled with them, and she afterwards told me: "Every morning before we all moved off from our hotel, I used to go along to the local supermarket, and there I would load up with fresh bread, a selection of cheese (Paul and Linda are both vegetarian), bottles of orange juice, jars of yoghurt, biscuits, lots of fruit, plenty of pickles (Paul likes pickles), and often fifteen bottles of beer for anyone who wanted a drink on the journey. Linda would always tell me if there was anything else they wanted—some special cheese or something like that, and then after I'd loaded up the bus with food and drink, off we'd go . . . The tour ran very smoothly, and the only unexpected thing that happened was Paul, Linda, me and several others got stuck in a lift at the Hotel Foresta in Stockholm. The lift suddenly stopped between the second and third floors. We all leaned to one side, putting our weight on the rail because Paul said that would take the weight off the centre, and gradually we rocked it back to the second floor. There was no alarm bell, so we couldn't let anyone know we were in trouble . . . we were stuck in there for fifteen or twenty minutes, and it got very hot and steamy, with the windows all steamed up. Afterwards it seemed very funny, but it was no good complaining because we'd got too many people in the lift."

Musically, the tour achieved what McCartney had set out to do; the band became used to playing before medium size audiences—which was an essential starting point for them if they were to go on to major international concert

116

tours as McCartney eventually intended (he had already been invited to take Wings on tour across the United States and also to Japan and Australia)—and those journalists who travelled over to Europe to see them were impressed, if not very wildly. "I like to see people leaping around and dancing and enjoying it, better than sitting there and analysing it," he said to Robin Denselow of *The Guardian*, who commented: "Certainly McCartney is too shrewd to let the new populist approach cause standards to drop; he is not letting the band play in Britain and (especially) America until it is good enough. 'I want to know that I'm ready, if there is a super-critical audience. This is no snub to Britain, but I don't like going in when I'm not ready. Doing this tour is like playing Hamburg eight hours a day with The Beatles.' . . . no doubt he also has in mind Lennon's unhappy experience at his first solo concert at Toronto (when he was literally ill with nerves) and so is taking entirely the opposite approach."

In the *Melody Maker*, Chris Charlesworth wrote: "He shakes his hips but the kids don't scream any more. His voice, whether screaming or singing, is everything it always has been, and his very presence commands a respect—even in France—few others could hope to achieve. And at the same time there's no doubt that he's thoroughly enjoying himself . . ."

After that tour, satisfied that Wings could now hold their own on stage, McCartney set the band to work on their next album. For nearly a year his work was mainly concentrated on either TV or recording studios—working on his ATV special for Sir Lew Grade's ATV, "James Paul McCartney," which was also shown across the USA; working on two other films which have never been released (one of them based on the European tour and telling the story of a mouse that travelled around with them on the coach; the other based on an idea that he asked me not to disclose); recording his hugely successful single 'My Love" and the theme song for the James Bond movie 'Live and Let Die," and the "Red Rose Speedway" LP, which was an international best-selling album in 1973. There was no doubt at all by then—when Wings made their first British tour—that McCartney had brought together a very fine band indeed. I saw them on stage at Oxford, and they were very good; musically, they were developing fast, even though there were still some rough edges.

"It's a very loose relationship . . ." Denny Laine told me then, "we plan our schedules around the kids' school holidays. We're recording and rehearsing when they're on holiday. Any family arrangements always come first. I've met all Paul's family up in Liverpool, and he's met all mine in Birmingham. They all come to our shows and then we have dinner afterwards . . . Paul will relax and take things easy, but the work always gets done. It's very disciplined, but still kept very loose."

Then just as it all seemed to be slotting gently into place, and McCartney was discussing offers that he had received to tour the United States and was planning to take the band to Lagos to record the "Band On The Run" album, the troubles began; Wings split, with Henry McCullough leaving after a musical dispute and Denny Seiwell announcing on the eve of their departure for Africa that he did not want to go.

Asked why he thought the others had left, Denny Laine told *Record Mirror*: "I really don't know why. Perhaps part of it was due to the pace that Paul works or perhaps it was because they felt their creativity was being stifled. If it was the latter then there was certainly no need for it because Paul has always encouraged us to contribute whatever we felt we could. He suggested that I write a song for the "Band On The Run" album, which was something I'd never thought of doing until then. I've always been the sort of person who writes when he's got nothing better to do . . . we want people to be involved totally in the band. They've got to believe in it. Paul, Linda and myself do. In fact perhaps that was part of the problem with Henry and Denny. They always appeared to act more like sidesmen than members of the band . . . Paul worked really hard at trying to keep the band together. He certainly never wanted either Denny or Henry to leave . . ."

McCartney himself explained to *Melody Maker* how

those musical differences with Henry McCullough had arisen: "It was actually that. We were rehearsing and I asked him to play a certain bit. He was loathe to play it, and kinda made an excuse about it couldn't be played. I, being a bit of a guitarist myself, knew it could be played, and rather than let it pass I decided to confront him with it, and we had a confrontation. He left rehearsals a bit choked, then rang up to say he was leaving . . . "

So the McCartneys and their children plus Denny Laine set off for Lagos, where they rented a couple of houses near the airport at Ikeja, about an hour's drive from the recording studios, joining a local country club so that they could always have somewhere to go for a swim. Each day they would start recording soon after 4 pm, and then work through until 10 pm—and sometimes until 4 or 5 am next morning, depending on how the music was going, and for nearly all the sessions—apart from when McCartney employed an African drummer—it was just the three of them, Denny, Linda and Paul.

The album that they recorded out there, "Band On The Run," was one of the most successful McCartney has ever been associated with—world-wide its sales are believed to be approaching 5,000,000, through it may be a year or two yet before all the sales can be calculated (and he did give Denny a percentage in the album).

Once they had returned to London, McCartney set about re-forming Wings—though at the time of writing none of the albums that he has recorded with the new line-up have been released. He is believed to have at least three albums in the can, though their release was delayed by the success of "Band On The Run." Likewise he still has material recorded with the previous Wings that has not been released, and those films, which quite possibly will not be shown now that the line-up is different.

In the place of Henry McCullough, he recruited Jimmy McCulloch. Although still only twenty years old when he was already one of the better-known British guitarists. He'd come down to London when he was just thirteen years old with the band One In a Million, he'd been a member of the group Thunderclap Newman who had a hit with the Pete Townshend-produced number "Something In The Air," and who had then worked as a guitarist with John Mayall—a position formerly held by Eric Clapton, Mick Taylor and Peter Green—before joining Stone the Crows and later Hugh Nicholson's group, Blue.

McCartney's choice of drummer was more surprising—it was the relatively unknown Geoff Britton, a karate enthusiast who represented Britain in the first karate international tournament with Japan, and who also holds a black belt. Britton had to undergo three auditions for his job with McCartney—and was one of fifty-two drummers at the first McCartney run-through. He had previously been with the Wild Angels, a moderately successful rock'n'roll revival group, and with East of Eden—and before joining McCartney had turned down jobs with Uriah Heep and Curved Air. "Working with McCartney is such an opportunity, such an eye-opener that you just can't afford to blow it. You can learn so much from him," Britton told *Melody Maker*.

With the new Wings, McCartney spent six weeks recording in Nashville during the summer of 1974—from which came the "Junior's Farm"/"Sally G" single released that autumn; and then went back into the studios in Britain throughout November, 1974, before starting recording again in New Orleans in January and February, 1975. They may stay together for some years, but there are no binding contracts that say they have to. Denny Laine is free to record another solo album if he wants to—and has plans to do just that. So, too, could Britton and McCulloch. Even Linda has her own recording plans with much material already completed at the time of finishing this chapter for an album under the name Suzy and the Red Stripes.

Thereafter, well—I shall be surprised if Paul McCartney does not at some time come back together again with John Lennon, George Harrison and Ringo Starr to record the occasional album, though he is hardly likely to break up Wings, for with them he now has the perfect vehicle for his own individual work, and a band to tour with when he feels the need to appear live before an audience, which is very important to him. This you may be sure he will continue to do because McCartney is, above everything else a working musician who just wants to carry on that way, reaching as large an audience as he can, whether it be as a Beatle again or performing with Wings.

Appendix

THE PAUL McCARTNEY CHRONOLOGY

Inevitably, this is also a Beatles chronology—because whatever else he may achieve for many Paul will always be a Beatle. And, anyway—as I suggest in this book—it is my belief that they will eventually work together again. This chronology is based entirely on my own Beatle files which date back to 1962 and tells in sequence how Paul and the others came together; what followed; how they parted, and what they each went on to do after that. It is as accurate as I can make it, with dates crosschecked where possible, and should help any serious fan or record collector put his (and their) career in perspective:

1940
7 July. Richard Starkey (Ringo Starr) born in Liverpool.
9 October. John Winston Lennon born in Liverpool.

1941
24 September. Linda Louise Eastman born in New York.

1942
18 June. James Paul McCartney born in Liverpool.

1943
25 February. George Harrison born in Liverpool.

1944
7 January. Michael McCartney (Paul's brother) born in Liverpool.
29 October. Denny Laine born in Birmingham.

1946

5 April. Jane Asher born in London.

1953

September. Paul enters Liverpool Institute High School.

1955

John Lennon, in his fifth year at Quarryback Grammar School, forms The Quarrymen skiffle group. Line-up changes frequently but includes Eric Griffiths on guitar, Pete Shotton on washboards and Colin Hanson on drums. Meanwhile George Harrison, who had been at the same primary school as John, moves on to the Liverpool Institute, forming his own group, The Rebels. Paul is at the same school where he stays until 1960, taking English Literature at Advanced level.

15 June. John and Paul first meet at a church fete in Woolton, Liverpool, where they are introduced by a mutual friend Ivan Vaughan, who was at school with Paul and already a friend of John. Paul plays with The Quarrymen on stage at the fete.

1956

31 October. Paul's mother, Mary Patricia McCartney, dies in Liverpool, aged 47.

1957

16 January. The Cavern Club opens in Matthew Street, Liverpool, as a jazz club.

1958

15 July. John Lennon's mother killed in Liverpool road accident.

29 August. George Harrison joins The Quarrymen at opening night of Casbah Club in Heyman's Green, Liverpool. The club was run by Mrs. Best, whose son Pete later became their drummer (though occasionally other drummers such as Johnny Hutch and Tommy Moore also played with them). Later that year, they change their name to Johnny and the Moondogs, later still to The Silver Beatles, while John and Paul appeared briefly as a duo

calling themselves The Nurk Twins. By now Lennon had left home to live in a flat in Gambia Terrace, near Liverpool College of Art where he was a student.

1960

April. As The Silver Beatles, with Pete Best on drums, they visit Hamburg for the first time—and are sent home when George is discovered to be under age. Throughout this period they play at Liverpool clubs and coffee bars—and at one time back a stripper in a strip club.

October. Two-week tour for Larry Parnes as Johnny Gentle's backing group. By now they are regularly a five-piece group with Stu Sutcliffe on bass.

December. Their second trip to Hamburg.

27 December. Special "Welcome Home" concert at Litherland Town Hall. Afterwards compere Bob Wooler writes in the local music paper "Mersey Beat": "The Beatles are the biggest thing to hit the Liverpool rock 'n' roll set-up in years . . ."

1961

21 March. The Beatles make their debut at The Cavern.

April. Their third trip to Hamburg, where they record with British singer Tony Sheridan for Polydor.

July. They begin appearing regularly every Wednesday night at The Cavern; soon they are appearing there two or three times a week and regularly at lunchtime sessions.

October. John and Paul holiday in Paris.

28 October. Epstein is standing in his record store in Whitechapel, Liverpool, when a boy, Raymond Jones, asks if he has a record called "My Bonnie" by a local group, The Beatles. Later two girls also ask for the record. Epstein tries to order copies, but finds it has not been released in this country. He mentions this to a friend—who tells him The Beatles appear regularly at The Cavern.

9 November. Epstein sees The Beatles for the first time at a lunch-time session at The Cavern.

3 December. Epstein invites The Beatles to meet him at his office over the record shop, having by now sold over a hundred copies of "My Bonnie" which he had imported. A few days later they sign their first contract with Epstein.

1962

1 January. The Beatles go to London for a recording test with Decca—and are turned down. Later they are also rejected by Pye.

January. The Star Club opens in Hamburg, and The Beatles are booked to play there the opening night. The same month they win their first award—as top group in a "Mersey Beat" popularity poll.

5 April. Special Beatles Fan Club Night at The Cavern before they leave for their fourth trip to Hamburg. Stu Sutcliffe, who had stayed on there after a previous visit, dies the night before they arrive for a seven-week season.

9 May. Brian Epstein sends a telegram to *Mersey Beat*, reading: "HAVE SECURED CONTRACT FOR BEATLES TO RECORDED (*sic*) FOR EMI ON PARLAPHONE (*sic*) LABEL 1st RECORDING DATE SET FOR JUNE 6th BRIAN EPSTEIN."

26 June. Brian Epstein's company Nems Enterprises Ltd. formed.

1 July. Appear at The Cavern with Gene Vincent.

August. Pete Best asked to leave The Beatles. Ringo takes his place—straight from Butlin's holiday camp at Skegness where he had been appearing with Rory Storm and the Hurricanes.

23 August. John Lennon marries Cynthia Powell at Mount Pleasant register office, Liverpool, with Paul McCartney as best man.

1 October. Beatles sign their second contract with Brian Epstein, appointing him their manager with effect from 1 October for a period of five years.

5 October. Their first single "Love Me Do"/"P.S. I Love You" released on Parlophone label.

25 October. Go to Manchester to record BBC Light Programme's "Teenagers' Turn" for transmission the following day.

26 October. Enter the *New Musical Express* chart for the first time, with the paper saying that when asked why they called themselves The Beatles they "laughingly put off this question by saying 'the name came to us in a vision.' "

28 October. Concert at Liverpool Empire with Little Richard, Craig Douglas and Jet Harris.

31 October. Leave for their fourth season in Hamburg.

1 November. Open at the Star Club, Hamburg, for fourteen days.

10 November. "Love Me Do" enters *Disc Weekly* chart at No. 28, rising to No. 24—and then vanishes.

17 December. Appear on "People and Places" (Granada TV) for a fee of £35. Producer Johnny Hamp says some years later: "I first saw The Beatles in a club in Hamburg. They were very scruffy characters—but they had a beat in their music which I liked . . . I got into a lot of trouble over it. Everyone said they were too rough, too untidy. But I liked them. I put them on again and again." (*Daily Mirror*—2 November, 1965.)

18 December. Begin another 14-day season at the Star Club, their fifth and last Hamburg club season.

30 December. Heather, Linda McCartney's daughter by her first marriage, born in the USA.

1963

1 January. Begin a tour of Scotland.

11 January. Their second single "Please Please Me"/"Ask Me Why"—their first No. 1 record—released on Parlophone label.

25 January. American record company Vee Jay, which had already had success with Frank Ifield, signs Beatles for US release—even though they have still not had a major British hit.

2 February. Begin their first nation-wide British tour at Bradford Gaumont, with Helen Shapiro top of the

bill. Also appearing were Danny Williams and Kenny Lynch.

11 February. In just twelve hours they record all the tracks for their first album, "Please Please me."

26 February. Northern Songs Ltd., their publishing company, formed with John Lennon, Paul McCartney, Brian Epstein and Dick James as directors. First song it published was "From Me To You."

7 March. "Please Please Me" LP released by Parlophone. Tracks: "Baby It's You," "Misery," "Anna," "Chains," "Boys," "Ask Me Why," "Please Please Me," "Love Me Do," "P.S. I Love You," "I Saw Her Standing There," "Do You Want to Know A Secret," "A Taste of Honey," "There's A Place" and "Twist and Shout."

9 March. Begin their second nation-wide British tour, this time at East Ham Granada with Tommy Roe and Chris Montez.

10 March. Birmingham Hippodrome.

12 March. Bedford Granada, and also appear on "Here We Go" (BBC Light Programme).

13 March. York Rialto.

14 March. Wolverhampton Gaumont.

15 March. Bristol Colston Hall.

16 March. Sheffield City Hall.

17 March. Peterborough Embassy.

18 March. Gloucester ABC.

19 March. Cambridge ABC.

20 March. Romford ABC.

21 March. Croydon ABC.

22 March. Doncaster Gaumont.

23 March. Newcastle City Hall.

24 March. Liverpool Empire.

27 March. Northampton ABC.

28 March. Exeter ABC, and also appear on "On The Scene" (BBC Light).

29 March. Lewisham Odeon.

30 March. Portsmouth Guildhall.

31 March. Leicester de Montfort.

8 April. John Charles Julian Lennon born at Sefton General Hospital.

12 April. Third single "From Me To You"/"Thank You Girl" released on Parlophone label.

April. The "Please Please Me" LP reaches No. 1 in the *New Musical Express* charts, where it stays for six months.

16 April. Appear on "6:25 Show" (BBC TV).

26 April. Billy J. Kramer debuts with "Do You Want To Know A Secret"/"I'll Be On My Way" (Parlophone). Both tracks written by Lennon and McCartney.

28 April. Appear in *New Musical Express* Poll Winners' Concert at Wembley Empire Pool, and afterwards leave for a twelve-day holiday in the Canary Islands.

9 May. Paul McCartney meets Jane Asher after a concert appearance at the Royal Albert Hall.

17 May. "Pops and Lennie" (BBC TV).

18 May. Begin third nation-wide British tour with Roy Orbison and Gerry and the Pacemakers at Slough Adelphi.

19 May. Hanley Gaumont.

20 May. Southampton Gaumont.

22 May. Ipswich.

23 May. Nottingham Odeon.

24 May. Harrow Granada.

25 May. Sheffield City Hall, and also appear on "Saturday Club" (BBC Light).

26 May. Liverpool Empire.

27 May. Cardiff Capitol.

28 May. Worcester.

29 May. York Rialto.

30 May. Kingston Granada.

31 May. Southend Odeon.

1 June. Tooting Granada.

2 June. Brighton Hippodrome.

3 June. Walthamstow Granada.

4 June. Birmingham Town Hall. Begin their own radio series "Pop Go The Beatles" (BBC Light).

5 June. Leeds Odeon.

7 June. Glasgow Odeon.

8 June. Newcastle City Hall.

9 June. End their tour with Roy Orbison at Blackburn St. George's Hall.

12 June. Liverpool charity concert at the Grafton ballroom in aid of the National Society for the Prevention of Cruelty to Children.

18 June. Paul McCartney's 21st birthday.

22 June. John records appearance on "Juke Box Jury" (BBC TV), then flies by helicopter to Abergavenny for ballroom appearance.

23 June. "Easy Beat" (BBC Light).

29 June. All-Liverpool edition of "Thank Your Lucky Stars" (ABC TV), and John Lennon's "Juke Box Jury" appearance screened the same evening.

8 July. Begin week at Margate Winter Gardens, appearing twice-nightly with Bill J. Kramer and the Dakotas.

16 July. "Pop Go The Beatles" radio series returns to the BBC Light for further ten weeks.

21 July. Concert at Blackpool Queens. Police called to control crowd of 4,000 in street outside. Beatles have to climb over the roof to get into the theatre.

22 July. Begin week at Weston Super Mare Odeon with Gerry and the Pacemakers.

26 July. Parlophone release "Beatles No. 1" EP with "Twist and Shout," "A Taste of Honey," "Do You Want To Know A Secret" and "There's A Place" with advance orders of 150,000. The same day Billy J. Kramer releases "Bad To Me," written by Lennon and McCartney (also Parlophone).

1 August. First issue published of *The Beatles Book,* the group's own monthly magazine.

3 August. The Beatles appear at The Cavern, Liverpool, for the last time—in a special Bank Holiday show with The Escorts and The Merseybeats.

6 August. Begin four-day booking at St. Helier Springfield ballroom, Jersey.

12 August. Begin week's appearance at Llandudno Odeon.

19 August. Begin week at Bournemouth Gaumont with Billy J. Kramer and the Dakotas and appear on "Scene at 6:30" (Granada TV).

23 August. Fourth single "She Loves You"/"I'll Get You" released on Parlophone label.

24 August. "Thank Your Lucky Stars Summer Spin" (ABC TV).

26 August. Begin week at Southport Odeon.

30 August. Brian Epstein launches Liverpool group The Fourmost with Lennon/McCartney song "Hello Little Girl" (Parlophone).

1 September. Record "Big Night Out" (ABC TV).

4 September. Begin brief tour with Mike Berry, Freddie Starr and the Midnighters at Worcester Gaumont.

5 September. Taunton Gaumont.

6 September. Luton Odeon.

6 September. Reported in *New Musical Express* that Epstein has signed his first girl singer, Cilla Black, and that she will debut on Parlophone with the Lennon/McCartney song "Love of the Loved." The same day Parlophone release a Beatles EP with the tracks "Please Please Me," "From Me to You," "Thank You Girl" and "Love Me Do."

7 September. "She Loves You" reaches No. 1 in the *Melody Maker* chart, a position it holds for a total of seven weeks. "Big Night Out" shown on ABC TV. They appear at Croydon Fairfields.

15 September. Concert at the Royal Albert Hall, London, and then they begin a sixteen-day holiday—with George flying to the States with his brother Peter to stay with their sister Louise in Benton, Illinois; John going to Paris and Paul and Ringo to Greece.

October. Parlophone release an EP with the tracks "I Saw Her Standing There," "Misery," "Anna" and "Chains."

5 October. Begin brief Scottish tour at Glasgow Concert Hall.

6 October. Kirkcaldy Regal.

7 October. Dundee Caird Hall.

9 October. Appear on BBC TV documentary "The Mer-

sey Beat," interviewed and seen at home in Liverpool as well as being shown on stage.

11 October. Announced that "She Loves You" has become their first Gold Disc with sales of over 1,000,000—and that sales of the "Please Please Me" LP have already passed 250,000. Appear that night at Stoke Trentham Gardens.

13 October. Top the bill on "Sunday Night At The London Palladium" (ATV). Fans riot in the streets surrounding the theatre—and the national papers discover Beatlemania.

15 October. Southport Floral.

18 October. Shrewsbury Music Hall.

20 October. In Birmingham to film "Thank Your Lucky Stars" (ABC TV)—and approximately 3,000 fans storm the studios.

24 October. Beatles fly to Sweden for five concerts and TV appearance.

26 October. Brian Epstein appears on "Juke Box Jury," and the Beatles' "Thank Your Lucky Stars" appearance (ABC TV) is also shown.

1 November. Begin British concert tour at Cheltenham Odeon with the Brook Brothers and The Kestrels.

2 November. Sheffield City Hall.

3 November. Leeds Odeon.

4 November. Triumphant appearance on Royal Variety Show at the Prince of Wales Theatre attended by Queen Mother, Princess Margaret and Lord Snowdon. Also on the bill were Marlene Dietrich, Tommy Steele and Max Bygraves. This was the night Lennon told the audience: "Those of you in the cheaper seats—clap your hands; and those of you in the more expensive seats—just rattle your jewellery."

5 November. East Ham Granada.

6 November. Northampton ABC.

7 November. Dublin Adelphi.

8 November. Belfast Ritz.

9 November. Slough Adelphi.

10 November. Birmingham Hippodrome.

12 November. Paul McCartney taken ill with gastric flu, and their concert at Portsmouth Guildhall is postponed.

13 November. Plymouth ABC, and the same evening BBC TV repeats their "Mersey Beat" documentary.

14 November. Exeter ABC.

15 November. Bristol Colston.

16 November. Bournemouth Winter Gardens—with three different film units preparing rival documentaries for American TV.

17 November. Coventry Theatre—with a photo-reporting team from the US magazine *Life*.

18 November. Presented with a silver LP for over 250,000 sales of "Please Please Me" by Sir Joseph Lockwood, chairman of EMI.

19 November. Wolverhampton Gaumont.

20 November. Manchester ABC—performance filmed for a cinema documentary.

21 November. Carlisle ABC.

22 November. Stockton ABC.

22 November. Their second LP "With The Beatles" released with advance orders of 300,000. Tracks: "All My Loving," "It Won't Be Long," "Hold Me Tight," "I Wanna Be Your Man," "Roll Over Beethoven," "Little Child," "Til There Was You," "Please Mr. Postman," "You Really Got a Hold On Me," "Devil In My Heart," "Not A Second Time" and "Money".

23 November. Newcastle City Hall.

24 November. Hull ABC.

26 November. Cambridge ABC.

27 November. York Rialto.

28 November. Lincoln ABC.

29 November. Huddersfield ABC. Their fifth single "I Wanna Hold Your Hand"/"This Boy" released by Parlophone with advance orders of 700,000.

30 November. Sunderland Empire.

1 December. Leicester de Montfort.

2 December. Charity show at Grosvenor Hotel, London.

3 December. Portsmouth Guildhall—concert arranged to

make up for their non-appearance on 12 Novem
ber when Paul was ill.

7 December. All four Beatles appear on "Juke Box Jury,"
screened by BBC TV from Liverpool Empire dur
ing their Northern Fan Club Convention. A film o
their show is featured on BBC TV that night titlec
"It's The Beatles"—and they also do two mor
shows at the Empire.

8 December. Lewisham Odeon.

9 December. Southend Odeon.

10 December. Doncaster Gaumont.

11 December. Scarborough Futurist.

12 December. Nottingham Odeon.

13 December. Tour ends at Southampton Gaumont. Re
ported in *New Musical Express* that they hav
signed with Capitol in the States, giving them firs
option for all future releases.

14 December. Southern Fan Club Convention at Wimble
don Palais—they shake hands with all 3,000 fan
there, and then perform on stage for half an hour
Every member of the Fan Club receives a speciall
recorded Christmas single.

21 December. The Beatles Christmas Show is previewed a
Bradford Gaumont.

22 December. Christmas Show preview at Liverpool Em
pire, and they are also seen in a special Christma
edition of "Thank Your Lucky Stars" (ABC TV)

23 December. Radio Luxembourg begins weekly serie
"It's The Beatles".

24 December. Twice-nightly Beatles Christmas Shov
opens at the Finsbury Park Astoria (until 11 Janu
ary). Also in the show are Cilla Black, Billy J
Kramer and the Dakotas and Rolf Harris as com
pere. After the first night Epstein charters a plane
so that they can all go home to Liverpool fo
Christmas Day.

26 December. Their own two-hour radio show on BBC
Light Programme.

27 December. The music critic of *The Times* says "th
outstanding English composers of 1963 must seer

to have been John Lennon and Paul McCartney ..."
and goes on to talk about the quality of their
"pandiatonic clusters."

1964

3 January. "I Wanna Hold Your Hand" goes to No. 1 in
Australia.

10 January. The Beatles crash into the US charts, with "I
Wanna Hold Your Hand" selling over 500,000
copies there in ten days, making it the fastest-ever
selling British disc in the States.

12 January. Their second appearance on "Sunday Night At
The London Palladium" (ATV).

14 January. In the States Capitol release the album "Meet
The Beatles," which includes tracks from both their
British LPs.

15 January. Make their French debut at Paris Olympia,
beginning a three-week season at the theatre.

17 January. In the States "I Wanna Hold Your Hand,"
coupled there with "I Saw Her Standing There,"
reaches No. 1 in the *Cash Box* chart. The *New
Musical Express* reports that in Britain alone The
Beatles have sold 7,000,000 LPs, EPs and singles
in the past year.

24 January. In the US *Cash Box* reports that the Beatles'
success is the main talking point of the American
recording industry and that this "could change the
whole thinking of American companies towards all
British records."

31 January. The *New Musical Express* reports that "She
Loves You" has now sold nearly 1,000,000 in the
US, that "I Wanna Hold Your Hand" has grossed
2,000,000 and that their "Meet The Beatles" LP
has already sold over 750,000.

February. In Britain Parlophone release the "All My Loving" EP. Other tracks: "Money," "PS I Love You"
and "Ask Me Why."

5 February. Return from Paris.

7 February. The *New Musical Express* reports that in the
US a group called The Swans have released "The

Boy With The Beatle Hair" (Cameo Parkway), Sonny Curtis has issued "A Beatle I Want To Be" (Colpix), a group called The Liverpools have brought out an LP "Beatle Mania in the USA" and The Buddies have released an instrumental single "The Beatles."

7 February. The Beatles fly to New York, where they find 3,000 fans waiting for them at Kennedy Airport plus over 100 photographers. There are riots outside their hotel, the Plaza, whose management say they would never have accepted the booking had they not thought Mr. Lennon, Mr. McCartney, Mr. Harrison and Mr. Starr were "four English businessmen."

8 February. From New York they have a radio interview with the BBC Light Programme's "Saturday Club," and then spend the day rehearsing for the "Ed Sullivan Show."

9 February. They debut on "The Ed Sullivan Show."

10 February. All-day session of press interviews.

11 February. Their first live US concert appearance at the Washington Coliseum with The Caravelles, Tommy Roe and The Chiffons. Afterwards they are the guests of the British Ambassador Sir David Ormsby Gore (now Lord Harlech) at a masked ball.

12 February. Carnegie Hall (tickets for both shows sold out in 24 hours).

13 February. They fly to Miami.

14 February. Day off.

15 February. Rehearse all day for their second appearance on Ed Sullivan's TV show.

16 February. Appear on "The Ed Sullivan Show" from the Deauville Hotel, Miami Beach.

18 February. They visit Cassius Clay (now Muhammad Ali) at his training headquarters, where he is preparing for the Sonny Liston fight.

21 February. Reported that The Beatles have been voted Show Business Personalities of the Year by the Variety Club of Great Britain.

22 February. Return from the US.

23 February. Film appearance on "Big Night Out" at ABC TV studios, Teddington—and in the States are seen for the third time on "The Ed Sullivan Show."

28 February. Polydor release "Cry For A Shadow," written by George Harrison and John Lennon and featuring Pete Best on drums, backed by "Why," sung by Tony Sheridan with backing by The Beatles. Both tracks were recorded in Hamburg in 1961.

29 February. Their appearance on "Big Night Out" screened by ABC TV, and Brian Epstein appears on "Juke Box Jury" (BBC TV).

2 March. The Beatles begin work on their first film "A Hard Day's Night," with location filming in Liverpool.

13 March. In the US trade paper *Cash Box* they are at No. 1 with "She Loves You," No. 2 with "I Wanna Hold Your Hand," No. 3 with "Please Please Me" and No. 4 with "Twist and Shout."

13 March. Reported that their American LP "Meet The Beatles has now sold over 3,600,000 copies—making it the biggest-selling album of all time. Well before release their next single "Can't Buy Me Love" has US advances of 1,700,000.

17 March. In Britain advance orders for "Can't Buy Me Love" go over 1,000,000.

20 March. Their sixth single "Can't Buy Me Love"/"You Can't Do That" released by Parlophone. They appear on "Ready, Steady Go" (Rediffusion TV) with Dusty Springfield.

23 March. Lennon's first book *John Lennon In His Own Write* published. Beatles receive two Carl Allen Awards—for being the most outstanding beat group of 1963, and for the most outstanding vocal record for dancing "She Loves You."

27 March. The first six records in the Australian Top Ten are "I Saw Her Standing There" (1), "Love Me Do" (2), "Roll Over Beethoven" (3), "All My

137

Loving" (4), "She Loves You" (5) and "I Wanna Hold Your Hand" (6).

30 March. Begin week at Liverpool Empire, and have their own Bank Holiday radio show on the BBC Light Programme. On BBC TV "Panorama" features a profile of Brian Epstein.

16 April. Ed Sullivan interviews them on the set of "A Hard Day's Night" at Twickenham Studios for his US TV show.

18 April. Appear on "Morecambe and Wise Show" (ATV).

23 April. John Lennon is the guest at a Christina Foyle Literary luncheon.

27 April. Begin two days' filming for Rediffusion TV show produced by Jack Good and also featuring Cilla Black.

29 April. Edinburgh (two concerts).

30 April. Glasgow Odeon.

6 May. Their "Around The Beatles" TV show screened (Rediffusion). Compered by US disc jockey Murray the K, and also featuring Millie, Cilla Black, Long John Baldry and P.J. Proby.

10 May. Radio Luxembourg broadcasts first half of programme "This Is Their Life."

15 May. "Love Me Do," only a minor hit in Britain 18 months earlier, reaches No. 1 in the US *Cash Box* chart.

17 May. Second half of "This Is Their Life" on Radio Luxembourg.

18 May. Their own Whit Monday Bank Holiday radio show on BBC Light Programme.

24 May. Ed Sullivan's film set interview and a clip from "A Hard Day's Night" shown on his US TV show.

29 May. Polydor release "Ain't She Sweet," sung by John Lennon, backed by The Beatles, another of their 1961 Hamburg tracks. The B-side "If You Love Me Baby" is sung by Tony Sheridan.

31 May. Two Sunday concerts at the Prince of Wales, London.

3 June. Ringo collapses in a Barnes photographic studio.

138

Jimmy Nicol deputises for him as they fly to Holland.

5 June. Dutch TV appearance.

6 June. Amsterdam—50,000 people throng the streets and canals as they tour the city. Concert in the auction hall at Blokker.

8 June. Fly to Hong Kong, stopping en route in Beirut, where fans try to clamber aboard the plane while they are sleeping. In Britain their Rediffusion TV special "Around The Beatles" is shown a second time.

10 June. Two performances at the Hong Kong Princess Theatre.

11 June. Ringo leaves University College Hospital.

12 June. Begin Australian tour at Adelaide, still with Jimmy Nicol on drums. Ringo flies out to join them and a crowd of 5,000 fans waits at Melbourne airport to greet him. In Melbourne a crowd estimated at 250,000 lines the streets to see The Beatles.

19 June. Parlophone releases "Long Tall Sally" EP. Other tracks: "Matchbox," "I Call Your Name" and "Slow Down."

19 June. Polydor releases an LP, mainly comprising tracks recorded by The Beatles with Pete Best as their drummer in Hamburg in 1961. The LP is titled "The Beatles' Firsts," Tracks are: "Ain't She Sweet" (with Lennon vocal), "Cry For A Shadow" (Lennon and Harrison instrumental), "Let's Dance" (Tony Sheridan and the Beat Brothers), "My Bonnie" (Beatles and Sheridan), "Take Out Some Insurance On Me Baby" (Beatles and Sheridan), "What'd I Say?" (Beatles and Sheridan), "The Saints" (Beatles and Sheridan), "Ruby Baby" (Sheridan and the Beat Brothers), "Why" (Beatles and Sheridan), "Nobody's Child" (Beatles and Sheridan) and "Ya Ya" (Sheridan and the Beat Brothers).

28 June. After a tour of New Zealand with concerts in Auckland, Dunedin and Christchurch they leave

for Brisbane for the final leg of their Australian tour.

2 July. Arrive back in London after their tour of Australia and New Zealand.

6 July. Princess Margaret attends "A Hard Day's Night" premiere at London Pavilion. Paul discloses that he bought his father a racehorse, Drake's Drum, for his birthday. "My father likes a flutter—he is one of the world's greatest armchair punters," he says.

8 July. "Top Of The Pops"—their first BBC TV appearance since the previous November.

10 July. Crowd estimated at 150,000 line Liverpool's streets when they return for a civic reception and the northern premiere of "A Hard Day's Night."

10 July. Their seventh single "A Hard Day's Night"/ "Things We Said Today" is released by Parlophone, and so is their LP "A Hard Day's Night" which includes the title track plus "I Should Have Known Better," "If I Fell," "I'm Happy Just To Dance With You," "And I Love Her," "Tell Me Why," "Can't Buy Me Love," "Any Time At All," "I'll Cry Instead," "Things We Said Today," "When I Get Home," "You Can't Do That" and "I'll Be Back."

12 July. George slightly injured when his E-type crashes in Chelsea. The group appears at Brighton Hippodrome, and in the States are seen again on "The Ed Sullivan Show."

15 July. ATV screen documentary "The Road to Beatlemainia."

16 July. The Beatles appear on "Brian Matthew introduces . . ." (BBC Light Programme).

17 July. Reported in the *New Musical Express* that Frank Sinatra, Sammy Davis, Bing Crosby and Dean Martin have recorded a parody of The Beatles for release on Sinatra's Reprise label—calling themselves The Bumblers. Also reported that US sales of "A Hard Day's Night" LP have reached 1,500,000—and are expected to reach 3,000,000

by early August and 5,000,000 by early September.

19 July. Star on "Big Night Out" (ABC TV) from Blackpool ABC.

July. John Lennon buys a £20,000 house at Weybridge; George buys a £20,000 bungalow at Esher, and Paul a five-bedroomed house for his father 15 miles outside Liverpool.

23 July. Beatles appear as waiters in a sketch in "The Night Of 100 Stars" charity show at the London Palladium.

25 July. George appears on "Juke Box Jury" (BBC TV).

26 July. Sunday concert at Blackpool Opera House.

28 July. Arrive in Stockholm with 3,000 fans waiting at airport.

29 July. Two concerts at Stockholm ice hockey stadium. While singing "Long Tall Sally," Paul gets an electric shock which makes his hair stand on end, and then John is thrown off his feet by another shock when he touches a microphone. "I felt a violent pain in my chest and sensed a flash in my head," says John.

30 July. Return to London from Stockholm.

31 July. Cilla Black releases single "It's For You," written by Lennon and McCartney (Parlophone).

1 August. Ringo appears on "Juke Box Jury" (BBC TV).

2 August. Sunday show at Bournemouth Gaumont.

3 August. Their own BBC Light Programme Bank Holiday radio show, and on BBC TV a programme on their making their first film is shown with the title "Follow The Beatles."

12 August. In the US "A Hard Day's Night" opens simultaneously at 500 cinemas.

16 August. Sunday concert at Blackpool Opera House.

18 August. Begin a 15,000-mile US tour, with 26 concerts in 18 States—and receive ticker-tape welcome and civic reception on arrival in San Francisco.

19 August. San Francisco Cow Palace.

20 August. Las Vegas Convention Hall.

21 August. Seattle Municipal Stadium.

22 August. Vancouver Empire Stadium.

23 August. Hollywood Bowl (two concerts, both recorded by Capitol. Seen in US on Ed Sullivan's TV show.

26 August. Denver Red Rocks Amphitheatre.

27 August. Cincinnati Gardens.

28 August. New York Forest Hills Tennis Stadium.

29 August. New York Forest Hills Tennis Stadium.

30 August. Atlantic City Convention Hall, New Jersey.

2 September. Philadelphia Convention Hall.

3 September. Indianapolis State Fair Coliseum.

4 September. Milwaukee Auditorium.

5 September. Chicago International Amphitheatre.

6 September. Detroit Olympia Stadium.

7 September. Toronto Maple Leaf Gardens.

8 September. Montreal Forum.

11 September. George Harrison forms his own song publishing company Harrisongs Ltd.

11 September. Jacksonville Gaitor Bowl, Florida—where they say they will not appear if the audience is racially segregated. "We all feel strongly about civil rights and the segregation issue," says Paul.

12 September. Boston Gardens.

13 September. Baltimore Civic Center.

14 September. Pittsburgh Civic Arena.

15 September. Cleveland Public Auditorium.

16 September. New Orleans City Park Stadium.

18 September. Dallas Memorial Coliseum.

19 September. Reported that they were now resting on a ranch in Missouri after earning £360,000 from the tour.

20 September. In the States they are seen on "The Ed Sullivan Show" on TV, and also appear at a New York charity concert.

October. Brian Epstein's book *A Cellar Full Of Noise* published by Souvenir Press.

9 October. The Beatles begin a four-week British tour with Mary Wells at Bradford Gaumont.

10 October. Leicester de Montfort.

11 October. Birmingham Odeon.

13 October. Wigan ABC.

14 October. Manchester Ardwick Apollo.

15 October. Stockton Globe.

16 October. Hull ABC. EMI issues "If I Fell"/"Tell Me Why" as an overseas single, and later make it available in Britain after dealers import copies— although it was never an official Beatles single. Beatles appear live on "Ready, Steady Go" (Rediffusion).

19 October. Edinburgh ABC.

20 October. Dundee Caird Hall.

21 October. Glasgow Odeon.

22 October. Leeds Odeon.

23 October. Walthamstow Granada.

24 October. Lewisham Odeon.

25 October. Brighton Hippodrome.

25 October. Announced that The Beatles have won five Ivor Novello Awards—for the most outstanding contribution to British music in 1963; for the most broadcast song ("She Loves You"), for the top selling record ("She Loves You"), for the second best selling record ("I Wanna Hold Your Hand") and for the second most outstanding song ("All My Loving").

28 October. Exeter ABC.

29 October. Plymouth ABC.

30 October. Bournemouth Gaumont.

31 October. Southend Odeon.

November. Parlophone release the "A Hard Day's Night" EP. Tracks: "I Should Have Known Better," "If I Fell," "Tell Me Why" and "And I Love Her."

1 November. Finsbury Park Astoria.

4 November. Luton Ritz.

5 November. Nottingham Odeon.

6 November. Southampton Gaumont.

7 November. Cardiff Capitol.

8 November. Liverpool Empire.

9 November. Sheffield City Hall.

10 November. Bristol Colston Hall.

November. Penguin publish "Love Me Do" by American

143

writer Michael Braun, which includes interviews with the group.

24 November. Paul's father, James McCartney, then aged 62, marries 35 years old Mrs. Angela Williams.

27 November. Eighth single "I Feel Fine"/"She's A Woman" released on Parlophone label. They appear on "Ready, Steady Go" (Rediffusion).

1 December. Ringo enters University College Hospital for a tonsils operation.

3 December. "Top Of The Pops" (BBC TV).

4 December. Parlophone release the "Beatles For Sale" LP. Tracks: "No Reply," "I'm A Loser," "Baby's In Black," "Rock and Roll Music," "I'll Follow The Sun," "Mr. Moonlight," "Kansas City," "Eight Days A Week," "Words of Love," "Honey Don't," "Every Little Thing," "I Don't Want To Spoil The Party" and "Everybody's Trying To Be My Baby."

In the Christmas newsletter, members of The Beatles Fan Club are told that membership has now risen to 65,000.

8 December. After going to see Spike Milligan in "Son of Oblomov," Paul tells the *Daily Express* that he plans to marry Jane Asher, but possibly not for two years. "When I marry, there will be none of this secrecy stuff. It just wouldn't work out," he says.

9 December. "Top Of The Pops" (BBC TV) (Filmed appearance).

10 December. Ringo leaves hospital.

18 December. EMI announce that the "Beatles For Sale" LP has sold nearly 750,000 copies in just Britain alone in two weeks.

24 December. Their twice-nightly Christmas stage show opens at Hammersmith Odeon. Also appearing are Freddie and the Dreamers, Jimmy Savile, Sounds Incorporated, The Yardbirds, Elkie Brooks and Ray Fell. The show runs to January 16.

All members of The Beatles Fan Club receive a special Christmas record.

26 December. Appear on "Saturday Club" (BBC Light Programme).

9 January. John Lennon appears on "Not Only . . . But Also" (BBC2), reading his poems.

19 January. Reported that four of the seven Gold Discs awarded in the US in 1964 were won by The Beatles—for "I Wanna Hold Your Hand," "Can't Buy Me Love," "A Hard Day's Night," and "I Feel Fine."

27 January. George Harrison is Best Man when his brother Peter marries his wife Pauline at Maghull, Liverpool; John Lennon is reported to be on a skiing holiday.

11 February. Ringo marries Maureen Cox at Caxton Hall. John and Cynthia Lennon and George Harrison attend the wedding, but Paul McCartney is in the USA.

18 February. Northern Songs Ltd. becomes a public company—the first song publishing company to be quoted on the London Stock Exchange. The shares are offered at 7s9d—and are ten times over subscribed.

22 February. Beatles leave for the Bahamas to begin filming their second film "Help!"

13 March. The "Help!" production team moves to Austria for location shooting before studio work at Twickenham.

20 March. Interviewed by phone from Australia on "Saturday Club" (BBC Light Programme).

1 April. Brian Epstein takes over the Saville Theatre, London, acquiring a controlling interest in the company that holds the lease.

3 April. Reported in *Mersey Beat* that the Pete Best Combo have broken up through lack of work. Paul and Ringo interviewed by Brian Matthew on "Thank Your Lucky Stars" (ABC TV) before the group performs.

9 April. Ninth single "Ticket To Ride"/"Yes It Is" released by Parlophone.

11 April. Appear at the annual *New Musical Express* Poll Winners' Concert at Wembley Empire Pool, and then later appear on "The Eamonn Andrews Show" (ABC TV).

14 April. The *Daily Express* reports that Paul McCartney has spent around £40,000 for a large Victorian house in Cavendish Avenue, St. John's Wood (which is still his London home). Also reported that McCartney sent a message to the Campaign for Nuclear Disarmament marchers, reading: "I agree with CND. They should ban all bombs. Bombs are no good to anyone. We might as well ban the bomb as be blown up by it."

15 April. "Top Of The Pops" (BBC TV).

18 April. Beatles seen in ABC TV film of the *New Musical Express* Poll Winners' Concert.

12 May. Finish work on "Help!"

4 June. Parlophone releases "Beatles For Sale No. 2" EP. Tracks: "Baby's In Black," "I'll Follow The Sun," "I Don't Want to Spoil The Party" and "Words of Love."

7 June. Beatles have their own two-hour Whit Monday radio show on the BBC Light programme.

12 June. The Beatles awarded the MBE. John Lennon says: "When my envelope arrived marked OHMS I thought I was being called up." Paul McCartney says: "I'm going to wear it in the garden."

14 June. War hero Paul Pearson, a former RAF squadron leader, sends back his MBE "because it has become debased." Former Canadian Member of Parliament Hector Dupuis sends back his MBE; former wartime anti-aircraft expert James Berg sends back his MBE; former naval officer David Evan Rees returns his OBE, and Mr. Cyril Hearn sends back his MBE.

17 June. Lt. Gen. Sir William Oliver, retiring British High Commissioner to Australia, says: "I think the Beatles deserve their MBE." Lord Netherthorpe says:

"They thoroughly deserve the award." Col. Frederick Wragg sends back his twelve medals to the Queen, and says that because of the award he is now no longer planning to leave an £11,000 bequest to the Labour Party in his will. "Is he leaving the money to us instead?" asks Lennon.

18 June. John Lennon appears on "Tonight" (BBC TV) talking about his new book *A Spaniard In The Works.*

18 June. Canadian Stanley Ellis and retired squadron leader Douglas Moffitt send back their MBEs.

20 June. Concert at the Palais de Sport in Paris (televised in France).

21 June. Author Richard Pape says he is returning his MBE as a protest against the award to The Beatles. He says: "If the Beatles and their like continue to debase the Royal honours list, then Britain must fall deeper into international ridicule and contempt."

22 June. Concert in Lyons.

24 June. Publication of John Lennon's second book *A Spaniard In The Works,* and he is interviewed on "Today" (ITV). First Italian appearance in Milan.

26 June. Genoa.

27 June. Rome.

28 June. Rome, and then they leave for the Cote d'Azur, staying at the Hotel Negresco where they hold a press conference.

29 June. Paul McCartney and George Harrison spend a day on a yacht owned by promoter Felix Marouani.

30 June. Concert at the Nice Palais des Fetes.

1 July. Fly to Madrid.

2 July. Concert in the Monumental bull ring, Madrid. Crowd of 10,000. Paul McCartney introduces their numbers in Spanish.

3 July. Another bull ring concert—in Barcelona with an audience of 18,000. In Britain John is heard interviewed in "World of Books" (BBC Home Programme) about *A Spaniard In The Works.*

4 July. Return to London, with 1,000 fans waiting to welcome them at London Airport.

17 July. Excerpt from "Help!" shown on 200th edition of "Thank Your Lucky Stars" (ABC TV).

23 July. Beatles' tenth single "Help!"/"I'm Down" released by Parlophone.

24 July. Reported that Ringo Starr had bought a £37,000 house at Weybridge.

29 July. Princess Margaret and Lord Snowdon attend "Help!" film premiere. Proceeds go to the Variety Club of Great Britain and the Docklands Settlement.

1 August. Appear on "Big Night Out" (ABC TV).

3 August. Announced that their company Subafilms is making a £60,000 colour film of the National Jazz Festival at Richmond on 6–8 August starring The Who, The Yardbirds, The Moody Blues, Georgie Fame, Manfred Mann, Spencer Davis and Rod Stewart. The film was later shown on American TV.

6 August. The "Help!" LP released by Parlophone. Tracks: "The Night Before," "You've Got To Hide Your Love Away," "Another Girl," "You're Going To Lose That Girl," "Help!," "Ticket To Ride," "It's Only Love," "Tell Me What You See," "I've Just Seen A Face" and "Yesterday" (all by Lennon and McCartney) plus two Harrison songs "I Need You" and "You Like Me Too Much" plus Larry Williams' "Dizzy Miss Lizzie" and "Act Naturally" by Vonnie Morrison and Johnny Russell.

John buys a bungalow near Bournemouth for his Aunt Mimi.

13 August. Reported in *New Musical Express* that Epstein had signed Paddy, Klaus and Gibson to a management contract. This was at The Beatles' request—Klaus Voorman was a close friend in Hamburg who works with them to this day; Gibson Kemp married Astrid Kirschner, who took some of their

first photographs in Hamburg and was Stu Sutcliffe's girlfriend until he died.

13 August. Reported that each Beatle had been insured for £1,000,000 prior to their US tour (London *Evening News*); another figure given was £2,000,000 each (London *Evening Standard*). They leave London for their third US tour.

14 August. Rehearse and record an appearance on "The Ed Sullivan Show" for US TV.

15 August. Concert at Shea Stadium—with an audience of 56,000. This was filmed and introduced by Ed Sullivan. They received 60 per cent of the gross, 160,000 US dollars—and were afterwards offered 350,000 US dollars to make a similar Shea Stadium appearance the following year.

15 August. Jane Asher tells the *Sunday Mirror*: "No, I am not Paul's wife . . . but yes, we are going to get married."

17 August. Toronto Maple Leaf Gardens (two shows).

18 August. Atlanta.

19 August. Houston.

20 August. Chicago.

21 August. Minneapolis.

22 August. Portland, Oregon.

23 August. Begin six-day stay in Los Angeles.

24 August. Northern Songs reported to have made profits for the year of £620,000.

28 August. San Diego.

29 August. Hollywood Bowl.

30 August. Hollywood Bowl.

31 August. San Francisco Cow Palace.

1 September. Return to London. Announced by EMI that their "With The Beatles" LP, released in November, 1963, has now sold over 1,000,000 copies in Britain alone.

September/October. On holiday.

7 September. London *Evening News* reports that Epstein has signed the Moody Blues to an agency and management contract.

13 September. Baby born to Ringo and Maureen Starr in

Queen Charlotte's maternity hospital, Hammersmith—named Zak.

25 September. In the US a weekly cartoon series based on The Beatles starts on TV.

1 October. Paul McCartney at No. 1 in both the major US charts—*Billboard* and *Cash Box*—with "Yesterday," the album track on which he was accompanied by a string quartet.

22 October. The *New Musical Express* reports that The Beatles declined invitation to appear in the Royal Variety Show. "It's just not our audience," says Paul McCartney, adding that they would donate the proceeds from one of their own shows to charity instead.

26 October. Beatles invested by The Queen with their MBE awards at Buckingham Palace.

1 November. Beatles record Granada TV special (see 1? December) with producer Johnny Hamp.

13 November. The *Melody Maker* reports that while in the US Epstein persuaded Capitol to withdraw a single "Boys"/"Kansas City"—because he felt it was not in their current style.

25 November. London store Harrods stays open for two hours after being closed to the public—so that The Beatles can buy their Christmas presents without being mobbed.

1 December. Parlophone release the "Rubber Soul" LP. Two Harrison tracks—"Think For Yourself" and "If I Needed Someone." Other tracks are by Lennon and McCartney—"Drive My Car," "This Bird Had Flown," "Nowhere Man," "Run For Your Life," "The Word," "Michelle," "Girl," "I'm Looking Through You," "In My Life," "Wait," "You Won't See" and "What Goes On," on which Ringo sings the vocal.

2 December. "Top Of The Pops" (BBC TV).

3 December. Parlophone release their eleventh single "Day Tripper"/"We Can Work It Out."

3 December. Beatles begin British tour at Glasgow Odeon

with The Moody Blues, The Paramounts, The Koobas, Beryl Marsden and Steve Aldo.

4 December. Newcastle City Hall, and appearance on "Thank Your Lucky Stars" (ABC TV).

5 December. Liverpool Empire—over 40,000 applications received for the 5,000 available tickets.

8 December. Sheffield.

9 December. Birmingham.

10 December. Hammersmith Odeon.

11 December. Finsbury Park Astoria.

12 December. Cardiff Capitol.

17 December. Granada TV screen their special based on the music of Lennon and McCartney—with Paul and Marianne Faithfull singing "Yesterday," Cilla Black singing "It's For You," Peter and Gordon singing "World Without Love," Billy J. Kramer singing "Bad To Me," Lulu singing "I Saw Him Standing There," Esther Phillips singing "And I Love Him," Richard Anthony singing "All My Loving" in French, and a 25-piece orchestra conducted by George Martin playing "I Feel Fine" and "Another Girl," plus a strings version of "She Loves You" by members of the Liverpool Philharmonic Orchestra and a jazz version of "A Hard Day's Night" by Alan Haven and Tony Crombie and Peter Sellers singing "A Hard Day's Night."

December. All members of The Beatles Fan Club receive their third Christmas single.

25 December. Paul McCartney quoted in *Record Mirror*: "I suppose I will marry Jane eventually. We've been going together for three years."

25 December. Beatles introduce special Christmas edition of "Saturday Club" (BBC Light).

1966

1 January. McCartney tells *Melody Maker* that Brian Epstein has "learned a lot in a very short time and is as straight as they come."

21 January. George Harrison marries Patti Boyd at Epsom register office. Paul McCartney was the only other

Beatle there. The Harrisons spend their honeymoon in Barbados.

28 January. Reported that Nems had taken over the Vic Lewis Organisation—bringing in Matt Monro and Donovan and making Brian Epstein the British representative of Tony Bennett, Herb Albert, Pat Boone, Trini Lopez, The Supremes, Johnny Mathis, etc. Vic Lewis says: "The merger makes us the biggest agency for live entertainers in the world."

4 February. Reported that in 1965 The Beatles had officially been awarded three US Gold Discs—for "Help," "Eight Days A Week" and "Yesterday."

28 February. The Cavern Club closes down on the orders of the Official Receiver, after a receiving order is made against Ray McFall. McFall says he has debts of £10,000 mainly through alterations and equipment for the club.

1 March. "Beatles at Shea Stadium" film shown on BBC TV.

March. Peter and Gordon release "Woman" by Bernard Webb, who is described as a student at a college in Paris—though it later turns out to be Paul McCartney, trying to see if the single would still be a hit if no-one knew who wrote it.

22 March. *Daily Express* reports that Paul McCartney and Jane Asher are on holiday at the Swiss skiing resort of Klosters.

25 March. McCartney tells the London *Evening Standard*: "We knew something would happen sooner or later; we always had this blind Bethlehem star ahead of us. Fame is what everyone wants, in some form or another . . . but we don't feel that famous. I mean we don't believe in our fame the way Zsa Zsa Gabor believes in hers."

26 March. Drake's Drum wins the Hylton Plate at Aintree at 20-1—and Paul McCartney leads his father's horse into the winners' enclosure.

5 April. Reported that Lennon and McCartney have each done a shares deal with Northern Songs netting

them each £146,000 in cash; that they had also each made another £94,000 by selling other shares—and that their shares in Northern Songs were now each worth £550,000.

18 April. Cavern Club sold by Trustee in Bankruptcy to confectioner and restaurant owner Joseph Davey of Wallasey for £5,500. The Beatles used to go to his café for chicken and chips in the early days. "I used to give them tea and bread and butter free as they were earning so little," he says.

April/June. Recording sessions.

1 May. Appear at the annual *New Musical Express* Poll Winners' Concert at Wembley Empire Pool—their last live stage appearance together as The Beatles in Britain.

14 May. The *Melody Maker* reports that they have sold over 1,000,000 records in Denmark which has a population of only four million people.

4 June. "Saturday Club" (BBC Light Programme).

5 June. Film sequences in London for inclusion in "The Ed Sullivan Show" on US TV.

9 June. Filmed appearance on "Top Of The Pops" (BBC TV).

10 June. Parlophone release their twelfth single "Paperback Writer"/"Rain".

11 June. Paul McCartney tells *Disc and Music Echo*: "I don't like our American image . . . I'd hate The Beatles to be remembered as four jovial mop tops . . . I'd like to be remembered, when we're dead, as four people who made music that stands up to being remembered."

16 June. Make surprise live appearance on "Top Of The Pops" (BBC TV)—their first live TV appearance since the previous August.

16 June. The *Daily Mirror* reports that in the US the sleeve for their American LP "Yesterday and To-day" has been withdrawn as "too offensive." The cover had shown The Beatles dressed in butchers' smocks, surrounded by chunks of meat, with the severed head of a doll.

17 June. The *Daily Mirror* reports that Paul McCartney is buying an 183-acre dairy farm near Machrihanish, Kintyre. Farmer's wife Mrs. Janet Brown said after Paul had gone there with Jane Asher: "Our farm has been up for sale for a while now but what a surprise my husband and I had when we saw the famous pair . . . Paul told me that it had always been his ambition to own a farm in Scotland."

18 June. "Thank Your Lucky Stars" (ABC TV).

22 June. Sibylla's discotheque opens in London—financially backed by George Harrison and Sir William Pigott-Brown. The Beatles and Rolling Stones are there on opening night.

23 June. Leave London Airport for Germany.

24 June. Two concerts at Munich Circus Kroner, with one video-taped for German TV.

25 June. Essen Grughalle.

26 June. Hamburg Ernst Merck Halle (two concerts).

27 June. Their jet from Hamburg forced to land at Anchorage, Alaska, to avoid typhoon in Japan.

30 June. Appear at the Martial Arts Hall in Tokyo, with afternoon concerts added for each day after 200,-000 ticket applications are received.

1 July. Martial Arts Hall, Tokyo.

2 July. Martial Arts Hall, Tokyo.

3 July. Arrive in Manila, Philippines—with 50,000 teenagers stopping all traffic to and from airport.

4 July. National Football Stadium, Manila—their largest-ever audience, estimated at 100,000. But they run into trouble when through a misunderstanding they fail to appear at a children's party at the President's Palace. This is taken as an insult to the President—and afterwards they are jeered, kicked and punched at Manila airport.

6 July. Go to New Delhi for three days' rest.

8 July. Return to London. Say they will never go back to the Philippines. "I wouldn't want my worst enemy to go to Manila," says Paul McCartney.

12 July. Lennon and McCartney win three Ivor Novello Awards for "We Can Work It Out" (top selling

single of 1965), for "Yesterday" (most outstanding song of the year) and also second award in best selling section for "Help!".

23 July. Prime Minister Harold Wilson re-opens the Cavern Club in Liverpool—with the Lord Mayor of Liverpool, Ken Dodd, the Liverpool and Everton football teams, Bessie Braddock, MP, and Jimmy Savile. The Beatles send a telegram.

29 July. Reported in the *New Musical Express* that The Beatles have turned down an offer to tour South Africa.

31 July. In Birmingham, Alabama, disc jockeys announce a bonfire of Beatles records and photographs as a protest against John Lennon's views on religion, which had first appeared in the London *Evening Standard*: "Christianity will go. It will go. It will vanish and shrink. I needn't argue about that. I'm right and I will be proved right. We are more popular than Jesus now. I don't know which will go first—rock 'n' roll or Christianity. Jesus was all right, but his disciples were thick and ordinary."

4 August. Beatles records banned by radio stations in Alabama, Ogdensburg (New York), Conroe (Texas), San Angelo (Texas), Salt Lake City (Utah) and Anderson (South Carolina) because of Lennon's remarks, which cause intense press controversy.

5 August. Parlophone release The Beatles' thirteenth single "Yellow Submarine"/"Eleanor Rigby"—the same day as the release of their "Revolver" LP. Of the fourteen LP tracks, eleven are by Lennon and McCartney—"Eleanor Rigby," "I'm Only Sleeping," "Here, There and Everywhere," "Yellow Submarine," "She Said, She Said," "Good Day Sunshine," "And Your Bird Can Sing," "For Noone," "Dr. Robert," "Got To Get You Into My Life" and "Tomorrow Never Knows." Harrison wrote the other three tracks—"Taxman," "Love You To" and "I Want To Tell You."

5 August. Cliff Bennett and the Rebel Rousers release "Got To Get You Into My Life"—produced by

Paul McCartney. "He played the number to me on the piano and showed me how to bend the notes," says Bennett.

6 August. In the US, thirty radio stations are now reported to have banned Beatles records because of Lennon's remarks. Epstein says: "John is deeply concerned and regrets that people with certain religious beliefs should have been offended."

6 August. Paul McCartney appears on the BBC Light Programme series "David Frost at the Phonograph."

11 August. Beatles leave for the US. In Chicago Lennon tells a reporter: "I am worried about what has been going on."

12 August. At a Chicago press conference, Lennon says: "I'm sorry. I'm sorry I said it, really. I never meant it as a lousy anti-religious thing . . . I am not a practising Christian, like I was brought up, but I don't have any un-Christian thoughts."

12 August. The Beatles' third and last major American concert tour opens at the Chicago International Amphitheatre.

13 August. Detroit Olympic Stadium.

14 August. Cleveland Municipal Stadium.

15 August. Washington.

16 August. Philadelphia Municipal Stadium.

17 August. Toronto.

18 August. Boston.

19 August. Memphis Coliseum. Ku Klux Klansmen picket the hall to protest at Lennon's religion remarks, and two firecrackers are thrown at them on stage.

20 August. Cincinnati.

21 August. St. Louis.

23 August. Return concert at Shea Stadium, again attended by 56,000 fans.

25 August. Seattle.

26 August. Paul McCartney denies rumours that he is planning to marry Jane Asher while they are in Los

Angeles. "It's absolute rubbish," he says. She says: "We're perfectly happy as we are."

28 August. Los Angeles Dodge Stadium.

29 August. The Beatles make what was to be their last appearance together as a group at San Francisco Candlestick Park.

31 August. They return to London. "We had a good tour, but it was all very tiring," says Paul McCartney.

19 September. Paul McCartney tells *Sunday Times*: "I don't think fans are humiliating themselves. I queued up at the Liverpool Empire for Wee Willie Harris's autograph. I wanted to do it. I don't think I was being stupid."

19 September. John Lennon flies to Spain to play the part of the soldier Gripweed in "How I Won The War," a film directed by Dick Lester.

20 September. Reported that George Harrison is in India, studying sitar with Ravi Shankar, and taking lessons in yoga.

24 September. Ringo forms Brickey Building Co. Ltd. with builder friend Barry Patience of Chelmsford.

13 October. Denny Laine leaves The Moody Blues.

14 October. Reported in *New Musical Express* that Paul McCartney was writing the musical score for the Hayley Mills film "Wedlocked or All In Good Time" (the title was later changed to "The Family Way."

24 October. Cardinal Cushing, Roman Catholic Archbishop of Boston, says he agrees that The Beatles "are more popular than Christ . . . the fact is that the group is better known than Christianity throughout the world."

14 November. Brian Epstein describes as "ridiculous" reports that Allen Klein has been approached over the future management of two of The Beatles. Klein's lawyer says: "It is quite true. Mr. Klein was approached through a third man on behalf of two of The Beatles."

15 November. Brian Epstein denies that The Beatles are splitting up and describes rumours to that effect as

157

"nonsense" when he attends the annual general meeting of Northern Songs Ltd.

19 November. Paul McCartney returns from a holiday in Kenya.

19 November. The *New Musical Express* says that the three Beatles in London were "aggravated" by the Klein report, and that Paul had been abroad and was probably unaware of the matter.

24 November. They start recording; their first work together since the US tour ended.

9 December. Parlophone release "Oldies (But Goldies)" LP, with one track previously unreleased in Britain—"Bad Boy," written by Larry Williams. Other tracks: "She Loves You," "From Me To You," "We Can Work It Out," "Help!," "Michelle," "Yesterday," "I Feel Fine," "Yellow Submarine," "Can't Buy Me Love," "Day Tripper," "A Hard Day's Night," "Ticket To Ride," "Paperback Writer," "Eleanor Rigby" and "I Wanna Hold Your Hand."

18 December. Premiere at the Warner Theatre for the film "The Family Way," starring John Mills and Hayley Mills with music by Paul McCartney, arranged by George Martin. This was the first time Paul was credited as a solo composer. He wrote twenty-six minutes of music for the film.

December. All Fan Club members receive Christmas single "Pantomime: Everywhere It's Christmas," Full colour sleeve designed and drawn by Paul McCartney.

26 December. John Lennon appears as lavatory attendant in a sketch in Peter Cook and Dudley Moore's "Not Only . . . But Also" (BBC2).

29 December. The US trade paper *Billboard* reports that The Beatles are currently No. 1 in thirteen countries.

31 December. Paul McCartney tells the *New Musical Express*: "Our whole outlook on life is changing because our circumstances have changed our surroundings . . . "

7 January. Reported that in 1966 The Beatles had again topped the US list of Gold Disc winners with six Gold Discs, according to the Record Industry Association of America.

8 January. The *Sunday Times* reports that Paul McCartney turned down an invitation from the National Theatre to write the music for the songs in Shakespeare's "As You Like It."

21 January. Nems Enterprises amalgamates with the Robert Stigwood Group bringing together The Who, Cream, The Merseys and Crispian St. Peters—though Epstein says he will continue to be personally responsible for The Beatles and Cilla Black.

30 January. Lennon and McCartney join Epstein in his box at the Saville Theatre to see The Who and the Jimi Hendrix Experience.

6 February. EMI announce that The Beatles have signed new nine year recording contracts and that their world record sales in converted single units (i.e. an LP being equivalent to six singles and an EP to two) now stand at over 180,000,000.

7 February. BBC-1 repeat the "Not Only . . . But Also" show in which John Lennon was seen as a lavatory attendant.

9 February. "Penny Lane" and "Strawberry Fields" film directed by Swedish film producer Peter Goldmann shown on "Top Of The Pops" (BBC TV).

16 February. The "Penny Lane" and "Strawberry Fields" films are repeated on "Top Of The Pops" (BBC TV).

17 February. Parlophone release The Beatles' fourteenth single "Penny Lane"/"Strawberry Fields Forever"—with the first 250,000 copies in a specially printed sleeve.

22 February. Northern Songs Ltd. predict annual profits for the year ending April of "not less than £810,000."

26 February. Reported that Epstein had bought a £35,000 house at Rushlake Green, East Sussex, that was used as a wartime rendezvous by Sir Winston Churchill and his Chiefs of Staff.

11 March. Announced that The Beatles have won two American Grammy awards—Lennon and McCartney for composing "Michelle," voted Song of the Year; Paul for best contemporary solo vocal performance on "Eleanor Rigby," Klaus Voorman also won a Grammy for his LP sleeve design for "Revolver."

11 March. Dick James tells *Disc and Music Echo* that already 446 different versions of "Yesterday" have been recorded.

25 March. The Beatles win two Ivor Novello Awards presented by the Songwriters Guild of Great Britain—for the most performed work of 1966 ("Michelle") and the best selling single of 1966 ("Yellow Submarine").

5 April. In Dallas, touring with the Bristol Old Vic, Jane Asher says: "I want to be known as a Shakespearean actress—not as Paul McCartney's girlfriend." Paul flies to Dallas to be with her on her 21st birthday.

7 April. Decca release Denny Laine's single "Say You Don't Mind"/"Ask The People" (Deram).

1 May. EMI announce that total world sales of Beatles' records have reached 200,000,000 (including an LP as equivalent to six singles and an EP as equivalent to two singles).

20 May. BBC bans "A Day In The Life" track from "Sgt. Pepper" LP because "it might encourage drug taking." Beatles deny that it has anything to do with drugs; and Lennon says: "The laugh is that Paul and I wrote this song from a headline in a newspaper. It's about a crash and its victim."

1 June. Parlophone release the "Sgt. Pepper's Lonely Hearts Club Band" LP, which had taken 700 hours to record. On George's song "Within You, Without You" he plays wtihout the other Beatles, accompanied by Indian musicians. All other songs are by Lennon and McCartney—"Sgt. Pepper's Lonely Hearts Club Band," "With A Little Help From My

Friends," "Lucy In The Sky With Diamonds," "Getting Better," "Fixing A Hole," "She's Leaving Home," "Being For The Benefit of Mr. Kite," "When I'm 64," "Lovely Rita," "Good Morning, Good Morning," "Sgt. Pepper's Lonely Hearts Club Band" (reprise) and "A Day In The Life." The sleeve design was by Peter Blake.

19 June. After the revelation in *Life* magazine that he had taken the hallucinatory drug LSD four times, Paul McCartney tells the *Daily Mirror*: "I don't regret that I've spoken out. I hope my fans will understand . . . "

21 June. After the drug-taking report, Dr. Billy Graham, the American evangelist, says: "I am praying for Paul that he finds what he is looking for . . . he has reached the top of his profession and now he is searching for the true purpose of life. But he will not find it through taking LSD."

25 June. The Beatles are seen on the "Our World" live TV programme by 400,000,000 people in 24 countries, who watch them in EMI studios recording "All You Need Is Love" with thirteen session musicians.

7 July. Parlophone rush-release "All You Need Is Love"/ "Baby You're A Rich Man," which is the Beatles' fifteenth single, after the success of the "Our World" show.

22 July. Paul McCartney tells *New Musical Express* that "All You Need Is Love" was written "in two weeks. We had been told we'd be seen recording it by the whole world at the same time. So we had one message for the world—'Love'. We need more love in the world."

24 July. Full page advertisement in *The Times* urging that "the law against marijuana is immoral in principle and unworkable in practice"—signed by all four Beatles together with Brian Epstein, authors, painters and politicians.

19 August. Jason Starkey, son of Ringo and Maureen, born.

27 August. *Sunday Express* reports that former Beatle Pete Best is working in a Liverpool bakery, slicing bread for £18 a week.

27 August. Brian Epstein found dead. Paul says: "This is a great shock. I am terribly upset." When his body was found, The Beatles were at a transcendental meditation course in Bangor, North Wales, with the Maharishi.

31 August. Reported in *The Times* that The Beatles are to become their own managers, and that Clive Epstein (now chairman of Nems) had said Nems would "give them every possible assistance in the conduct of their affairs."

2 September. Paul McCartney tells the *New Musical Express* that they will not appoint another manager. "No-one could possibly replace Brian," he says.

11 September. Work begins on the "Magical Mystery Tour" film with a coach trip to Devon, Somerset and Cornwall and scenes on an airfield at West Malling, Kent.

7 October. Reported that Ringo Starr is to have a solo acting role in the Hollywood film "Candy"—and that The Beatles have turned down a million-dollar offer from US promoter Sidney Bernstein to play two concerts at Shea Stadium.

13 October. "How I Won The War" by Musketeer Gripweed and the Third Troop is released by United Artists. It is largely instrumental, but John Lennon (who played Gripweed in the film "How I Won The War") can be heard on the disc.

17 October. Rolling Stones deny that they are forming a business partnership with The Beatles. Press statement reads: "Mick Jagger states that preparatory conversations of a purely exploratory nature were held between himself and Paul McCartney . . . " and goes on to say they had considered opening a jointly owned studio, but had not proceeded with the idea.

18 October. Premiere of "How I Won The War," the Dick

Lester film in which John Lennon played his first solo role.

7 November. Three portraits of Paul McCartney included in John Bratby exhibition at the Zwemmer Gallery, each with a £350 price tag. Reported that McCartney had a two hour sitting at Bratby's studio.

10 November. Spend the day filming "Hello Goodbye" film clips at the Saville Theatre, with Paul McCartney directing.

23 November. The film clips, with them wearing Sgt. Pepper uniforms, are banned by two BBC TV programmes ("Top Of The Pops" and "Late Night Line Up") because of a Musicians Union ruling on miming.

24 November. Parlophone release The Beatles' sixteenth single "Hello Goodbye"/"I Am The Walrus."

1 December. The "Magical Mystery Tour" EP package released by Parlophone—containing a 32-page cartoon book and two discs, each with three tracks. One number is "Flying," a wholly non vocal track written by all four members. Other tracks: "Fool On The Hill," "Your Mother Should Know," "I Am The Walrus," "Magical Mystery Tour" and Harrison's "Blue Jay Way."

2 December. After reports that a chain of "Sgt. Pepper's Lonely Hearts Clubs" is being opened across the States, Nems press officer Tony Barrow says: "One of the Beatles' companies is discussing this project, but I have nothing to say beyond this."

4 December. The Apple boutique opens in Baker Street, London, managed by Pete Shotton, a one-time member of The Quarrymen. Ringo flies to Rome to begin filming "Candy" in which he plays a Mexican gardener.

11 December. On holiday with Jane Asher at his Scottish farm, Paul McCartney says: "We shall get married . . . I think everyone knows this. But when we don't know." All members of Beatles Fan Club receive Christmas disc with sleeve design by John's five year old son Julian.

163

26 December. "Magical Mystery Tour" shown on BBC TV, who are reported to have paid £20,000 for screening rights. Critics slate the film, which is seen by 13,000,000 viewers. The *Daily Mirror* says: "If they were not The Beatles, the BBC would not have fallen for it."

27 December. McCartney, who directed the film, tells the *Evening Standard*: "We goofed, really. My Dad brought the bad news into me this morning like the figure of doom. Perhaps the newspapers are right—perhaps we're right. We'll have to wait and see."

27 December. McCartney appears on "The Frost Programme" (ITV) and says he thought "the film was badly received because people were looking for a plot . . . but there wasn't one."

1968

5 January. "Magical Mystery Tour" repeated on BBC TV.

6 January. The *Daily Telegraph* reports that Epstein left £486,032 (£266,032) net and that letters of administration have been granted to his mother.

6 January. Reported in the *Daily Mirror* that John Lennon has ended the family feud with his father, Alfred (55), who left home when John was a child. "From now on I hope we'll be in close contact all the time," says John.

19 January. First Apple group—Grapefruit—launched with the single "Dear Delilah." Their name was chosen by Lennon.

30 January. Cilla Black begins BBC TV series, opening and closing the shows with a specially written Paul McCartney song "Step Inside Luv," which is subsequently released as a Cilla single.

5 February. McCartney appears at a press conference at the Royal Garden Hotel, London, to publicise the Leicester Arts Festival—at the request of a student who talked his way into McCartney's home claiming to be a friend.

10 February. "Magical Mystery Tour" shown on Dutch

TV, after executives say "the quality was not as bad as we had been led to believe."

10 February. Paul McCartney and Jane Asher go to the Queen Elizabeth Hall to see his brother Mike McGear appearing with Scaffold.

24 February. McCartney tells the *Evening Standard*: "Instead of trying to amass money for the sake of it we're setting up a business concern at Apple—rather like a Western Communism . . . we've got all the money we need. I've got the house and the cars and all the things that money can buy."

February/April. All four Beatles, their wives and Jane Asher go to India for a course with the Maharishi, where they are also joined by Mia Farrow and Mike Love of the Beach Boys.

9 March. "Sgt. Pepper" LP wins four US Grammy awards— as Best Album of the Year, Best Contemporary Album, Best Engineered Recording and for the Best Album Cover.

15 March. Parlophone release their seventeenth Beatles single "Lady Madonna," coupled with "Inner Light," the first Harrison song to be featured on a Beatles single. This was The Beatles' last single on The Parlophone label.

7 April. Reported that The Beatles have sold "Magical Mystery Tour" for showing on Japanese TV.

20 April. Apple advertises in the *New Musical Express* that they want to help unknown songwriters and musicians. Paul says: "It's ridiculous that people with talent like Dave Mason and Denny Laine have sometimes had to struggle to get their work accepted . . ."

30 April. Paul McCartney in Bradford conducting the Black Dyke Mills Band playing "Thingumybob," a theme tune he had written for a London Weekend TV comedy series.

5 May. Twiggy sees Mary Hopkin on "Opportunity Knocks"—and tells McCartney about her. He phones Mary Hopkin, and suggests she records for Apple.

15 May. John Lennon and Paul McCartney, who are visiting the States to launch Apple, hold a pres conference—where Paul meets Linda Eastma again. John and Paul also appear on "Tonight" (NBC TV).

21 May. Paul McCartney and Jane Asher lunch with Andy Williams and then later attend his concert a the Royal Albert Hall—and go on to a party with him afterwards.

22 May. John and Yoko and George and Patti Harrison attend press preview for Apple Tailoring (Civil and Theatrical) which opens the following day in the Kings Road, Chelsea.

8 June. Paul McCartney and Jane Asher attend his brother Mike's wedding at Carrog, Merioneth, to hair stylist Angela Fishwick.

8 June. In a *Melody Maker* interview, McCartney discloses that The Beatles wrote twenty songs while in India with the Maharishi.

20 June. The London *Evening Standard* reports that The Beatles have reached agreement with Capitol in the US and with EMI in Britain that their future records will be released on the Apple label, and that for the next three years those companies would also distribute all Apple products.

22 June. The *New Musical Express* reports that Paul McCartney has filmed an hour long interview with David Frost for US TV.

22 June. Reported in the *Daily Telegraph* that Apple had bought 3 Savile Row, former headquarters of the Jack Hylton Organisation, with about 12,000 square feet, for £500,000.

22 June. Lennon appears on "Release" (BBC 2), talking about the stage adaptation of *In His Own Write* and *A Spaniard In The Works*.

1 July. Lennon "happening" at the Robert Fraser Gallery—John and Yoko appear dressed in white, "plight their troth," and let off balloons carrying messages to those who find them. "I declare these balloons high," says Lennon.

7 July. Reported that Patti Harrison is opening a stall in Chelsea Antique Market, specialising in art nouveau.

8 July. Apple subsidise children's beach show at Brighton, presented by actor David Peel under the title Apple Peel. He says: "I approached Paul with the idea and he agreed to help straight away, as well as suggesting our title . . ."

17 July. Paul McCartney arrives alone to join John and Yoko and Ringo and Maureen at the world premiere of "Yellow Submarine" cartoon film at the London Pavilion, and then they go on to a party at the Royal Lancaster Hotel.

20 July. Appearing on "Dee Time" (BBC TV), Jane Asher says that her engagement to Paul McCartney was off—but that she had not broken it. She said they had been engaged seven months since Christmas Day after knowing each other five years.

21 July. Jane says of her broken romance: "I don't want to say anything about it." (*Sunday Mirror*.) Paul's father tells *The People*: "Paul has never given any hint that he and Jane were parting. They were a really happy couple at their engagement party last Christmas."

30 July. Paul McCartney says: "We decided to close down the shop last Saturday—not because it wasn't making any money, but because we thought the retail business wasn't our particular scene. So we went along, chose all the stuff we wanted—I got a smashing overcoat—and then told our friends. Now everything that is left is for the public . . ."

31 July. All the stock given away at the Apple boutique in Baker Street. Crowds camp out all night. The value of the stock is estimated at £20,000.

31 July. The *Daily Telegraph* reports that McCartney's home is among those that are to be subject to a preservation order in St. John's Wood as a group

of houses "having special architectural or histori interest."

1 August. After widespread criticism of their manage ment of the Apple boutique affair, Paul McCar ney tells the *Daily Mail*: "We always make ou mistakes in public."

2 August. London Weekend TV comedy series "Thingu mybob" starts, starring Stanley Holloway, with th theme tune written by McCartney and played b the Black Dyke Mills Band.

3 August. Reported in *Disc and Music Echo* tha McCartney has been seen with a girl called Fran a the Revolution club. Apple spokesman Derek Tay lor says: "I don't know anything about the boys personal affairs."

7 August. In the early hours McCartney and friends go t the empty Apple boutique, slap white paint ove the windows—tracing the words "Hey Jude" an "Revolution." Paul tells the *Evening Standard* "We thought we'd paint the windows for a gas What would you do if your shop had just closed?"

11 August. Apple record label launched with Nationa Apple Week—and the release of "Thingumybob" by the Black Dyke Mills Band, conducted by Pau McCartney, and George Harrison's "Wonderwall" LP.

16 August. Apple releases "Those Were The Days," b Mary Hopkin, produced by Paul McCartne (which sold 4,000,000 copies world-wide in fou months).

23 August. Reported that Cynthia Lennon was suin John Lennon for divorce, citing Yoko Ono.

24 August. Ronan O'Rahilly, formerly boss of Radi Caroline, joins Apple as "business adviser." Pres officer Derek Taylor says: "John admires hin very much for what he did with Radio Caroline.'

30 August. Apple releases The Beatles' eighteenth singl "Hey Jude"/"Revolution," which is their first o the Apple label.

30 August. Former road manager Neil Aspinall, now Ap

ple managing director, marries Susan Ornstein at Chelsea register office.

8 September. The Beatles appear on "Frost On Sunday" (London Weekend TV) singing "Hey Jude."

14 September. Reported in *New Musical Express* that "Hey Jude" had already grossed sales of 2,000,-000.

14 September. Paul McCartney tells *Melody Maker*: "I'd love to produce an album for Elvis. His albums haven't been produced very well and as I am a fan of his I think I'd be able to produce him well."

"All My Loving" documentary, produced and directed by Tony Palmer, first shown on BBC-1.

The Hunter Davies official biography of The Beatles published by Heinemann.

12 October. Jane Asher tells *Evening Standard*: "I know it sounds corny but we're still very close friends. We really are. We see each other and we love each other, but it hasn't worked out. That's all there is to it. Perhaps we'll be childhood sweethearts and meet and get married again when we're about seventy."

18 October. Police raid flat in Montagu Square, Marylebone, where John and Yoko are living, and they are remanded on bail at Marylebone Magistrates Court on a charge of possessing a dangerous drug—cannabis.

28 October. Divorce petition by Cynthia Lennon officially listed.

8 November. John Lennon and Yoko Ono take full advertisement in music papers to advertise an appeal for "The Peace Ship," an independent and neutral radio station which will be broadcasting to both sides in the Middle East.

8 November. Cynthia Lennon granted her divorce.

9 November. Reported that George Harrison has not renewed his contract with Northern Songs, which had expired in March.

9 November. John Lennon releases his "Two Virgins"

LP with photos of himself and Yoko Ono nude on the cover.

16 November. Reported in *New Musical Express* that Lennon and McCartney had had discussions with Lord Beeching to see if he would run Apple for them.

21 November. Yoko Ono loses her baby at Queen Charlotte's Maternity Hospital, London, with John at her bedside.

24 November. Grapefruit leave Apple and manager Terry Doran tells *The People*: "I like The Beatles as friends, but not bosses . . . there is too much driftwood at Apple."

28 November. "Yellow Submarine" LP released with four new songs written for the film—"Hey Bulldog," "Northern Song" (George Harrison), "All Together Now" and "All Too Much." Also on this LP were "All You Need Is Love" plus the title track and six re-recorded tracks of incidental music played by George Martin and his Orchestra.

28 November. John Lennon fined £150 with twenty guineas costs after he had admitted possessing cannabis resin. On being questioned after the raid, he was said to have asked: "Can I just ask a question? As this stuff is all mine it will be me only who is involved?" His solicitor told the court that after the raid, Yoko had lost her baby, which had been an awful blow to them.

30 November. The Beatles' double album—the "white album"—released by Apple. Tracks: "Back In The USSR," "Dear Prudence," "Glass Onion," "Ob-La-Di, Ob-La-Da," "Wild Honey Pie," "The Continuing Story of Bungalow Bill," "While My Guitar Gently Weeps," "Happiness Is A Warm Gun," "Martha My Dear," "I'm So Tired," "Blackbird," "Piggies," "Rocky Raccoon," "Don't Pass Me By," "Why Don't We Do It In The Road," "I Will," "Julia," "Birthday," "Yer Blues," "Mother Nature's Son," "Everybody's Got Something To Hide Except Me and My Monkey," "Sexy Sadie,"

"Helter Skelter," "Long, Long, Long," "Revolution 1," "Honey Pie," "Savoy Truffle," "Cry, Baby, Cry," "Revolution 9" and "Good Night."

30 November. The *New Musical Express* reports that sales of "Hey Jude" are now approaching 6,000,-000 world wide.

7 December. Reported in *Disc and Music Echo* that Paul McCartney has a new girlfriend Linda Eastman, a photographer whose work had appeared in *Rolling Stone* and *The New York Times*. "Rumours first began to circulate that she and Paul were good friends about two weeks ago when Paul came to New York for a few days," says their American correspondent.

18 December. Another Lennon "happening"—this time at the Royal Albert Hall, London, where he and Yoko appear on stage, writhing inside a large white bag.

December/January. John and Yoko produce their film "Rape" for Austrian TV. In the film a girl is hounded by cameras until she is near to tears. "We are showing how all of us are exposed and under pressure in our contemporary world . . . what is happening to this girl on the screen is happening in Biafra, Vietnam, everywhere," says Lennon.

1969

18 January. Lennon tells *Disc and Music Echo*: "Apple is losing money. If it carries on like this, we'll be broke in six months." He also tells Dutch TV: "I used to have a lot, but suddenly I am the poorest Beatle . . ."

8 February. Reported that Allen Klein had been appointed by The Beatles to look into their business affairs. Lennon says: "We know him through Mick Jagger and we trust him—as much as we trust any businessman."

21 February. Mary Hopkin releases LP "Post Card" with Paul McCartney and Donovan playing guitar on several tracks. The sleeve was designed by Paul, who suggested the title—and his hand written list

171

of tracks is on the reverse of the LP cover. Paul suggested one track "Honeymoon Song," which he used to sing at The Cavern. Photos are by Linda Eastman.

March/May. Ringo makes his second film, "The Magic Christian," in which he appears as Peter Sellers' adopted son.

12 March. Paul McCartney marries Linda Eastman at Marylebone Register Office with his brother Mike and Beatles road manager Mal Evans as witnesses. Afterwards the couple go to St. John's Wood Church for a blessing by the Rev. Noel Perry-Gore. The night before the wedding Paul recorded Jackie Lomax singing "Thumbin' A Ride," which Paul had found on the B-side of a Coasters' record in his own collection. Also on the session were George Harrison and Billy Preston. On his wedding night Paul returned to the studio to finish off the Lomax track.

12 March. While George is working at the studios, police raid his Esher home where Patti is alone. George returns there and they are arrested and bailed on a cannabis charge.

16 March. Paul and Linda McCartney fly to New York with Heather, Linda's daughter by her first marriage, to spend three weeks with Linda's family.

March. Dick James sells all his shares in Northern Songs to ATV, who announce that they wish to buy a controlling stake in the company.

20 March. John and Yoko, on holiday in Paris, make a half-day trip to Gibraltar, where they marry with Peter Brown and David Nuttall of Apple as witnesses.

21 March. Reported in the *Financial Times* and the *Daily Telegraph* that Allen Klein has now been appointed business manager for The Beatles under a three year contract. Klein tells the *Telegraph* that he will receive 20 per cent of all money collected by Apple but not 20 per cent of money due under their existing recording contracts, though he would

receive 20 per cent of any increase he negotiated on those contract figures.

26 March. John and Yoko begin their peace bed-in at the Amsterdam Hilton. "Can you think of a better way to spend seven days. It's the best idea we've had," says Lennon.

28 March. Mary Hopkin releases "Goodbye," written by McCartney who also sang duet and played guitar. It was coupled with "Sparrow" and released simultaneously by Apple in 28 countries with promotional film showing Paul and Mary making the record.

31 March. George and Patti Harrison both fined £250 for illegally having cannabis at their home. "I hope the police will leave us alone now," says George afterwards

1 April. Lennon tells the *Daily Express*: "I am back to work, recording with The Beatles—I need the money . . . I'm scratching the deck, to my way of thinking. Right now in cash I have about £50,-000."

3 April. The *New Musical Express* reports that Billy Preston has signed with Apple, and that George Harrison is producing him.

5 April. The *Financial Times* reports: "It appears that Dick James, managing director of Northern Songs, has failed to persuade Beatles John Lennon and Paul McCartney to accept the £9,000,000 bid for Northern from ATV."

10 April. The Beatles reject the ATV offer and say they are consulting experts "with a view to making a counter-bid." Sir Lew Grade of ATV tells the *Daily Telegraph*: "We have 35 per cent of the shares and we will not let go of that for anything."

18 April. Apple releases The Beatles' nineteenth single "Get Back"/"Don't Let Me Down," which features Billy Preston on piano—the first time another artist had appeared on one of their singles. They had known Preston since their Hamburg days when he was over there with Little Richard.

19 April. The *New Musical Express* reports that in its first four months Apple had grossed world sales of £1,400,000.

19 April. Reported that Beatles and advisers, merchant bankers Henry Ansbacher, have agreed on the basis for a rival bid for control of Northern Songs. Sir Lew Grade says he is not considering raising the ATV offer.

25 April. John and Yoko's film "Rape" shown at the Montreux TV festival where the German entry is "Hippie Happy Yeah," which has Beatle songs as its music.

25 April. The Beatles offer 42s 6d cash per share for the 20 per cent they need to get control of Northern Songs (which would have meant an outlay of £2,-100,000).

26 April. John Winston Lennon changes his middle name to Ono in a ceremony before a Commissioner of Oaths on the roof of the Apple building in Savile Row.

26 April. Paul McCartney debunks rumours that he is dead. "I'm as fit as a fiddle," he tells reporters who visit his Scottish farm.

26 April. Jane Asher's father Dr. Richard Asher found dead at his home in Wimpole Street, and the Coroner later decides his death was due to self-administered barbiturates coupled with the effects of alcohol.

30 April. In the year up to April 30, it was subsequently reported that Northern Songs made pretax profits of £1,164,728. Beatles say that if they win control of Northern Songs, ATV will be asked to nominate a director. "I've enjoyed it all very much—it's Monopoly," Lennon tells the *Daily Telegraph*.

1 May. Apple release John and Yoko's "Unfinished Music No. 2—Life with The Lions" LP on their new Zapple label. The tracks include a recording of the heartbeat of the baby that Yoko was carrying prior to her miscarriage.

2 May. ATV claim that they now have support from

shareholders holding 45 per cent of Northern Songs' shares—and extend their offer up to 15 May.

3 May. Apple releases the George Harrison LP "Electronic Sounds" (Zapple).

4 May. Ringo Starr and Peter Sellers host a party at Les Ambassadeurs to celebrate completion of "The Magic Christian." Guests include Paul and Linda McCartney, John and Yoko, Richard Harris, Roger Moore, Sean Connery, Stanley Baker, Christopher Lee, George Peppard and Spike Milligan.

5 May. Reported that John and Yoko have bought Tittenhurst Park, Ascot, a Georgian mansion with 72 acres of land, for £145,000, and are planning to move in during August.

8 May. Reported that The Beatles have sacked Apple general manager Alistair Taylor, who was Epstein's personal assistant eight years earlier. "It was a hell of a blow," he says. Paul McCartney tells the *Daily Express*: "It is not possible to be nice about giving someone the sack."

19 May. Lennon and McCartney receive the Ivor Novello Award for "Hey Jude," the top selling British song in 1968.

20 May. Apple release The Beatles' twentieth single, and the last one that John Lennon and Paul McCartney recorded together—"The Ballad of John and Yoko," on which they were the only members playing with Paul on drums and piano and John on guitar. The coupling was "Old Brown Shoe."

6 June. Reported in *The Western Times and Gazette* that Paul and Linda McCartney had been househunting in Devon, and had viewed the 4,600-acre Emmetts Grange estate which was for sale at around £200,000.

July. John Lennon and the Plastic Ono Band release "Give Peace A Chance," which they had recorded in Montreal, with "Remember Love" (Apple).

July. John and Yoko are detained in hospital after being

injured in a road accident in Scotland, and the
they charter a jet to fly back to London.

28 August. Mary McCartney, daughter of Paul an
Linda, born in a London nursing home.

September. John and Yoko release their "Wedding A
bum," boxed with photos of the wedding (Apple)

5 September. Reported in the *Daily Telegraph* that Alle
Klein had re-negotiated The Beatles' existing con
tracts with EMI in the US, Canada and Mexico
subject to their recording a minimum of two a
bums a year until 1976. "If they do, all new a
bums will earn them 58 cents each during the nex
three years and 72 cents to 1972. This compare
with around 6 cents per album before 1966 and 3
cents in 1966/69. Reissues of the earliest record
ings will now attract a 56 cent royalty until 197
and 72 cents after that," said the *Daily Tele
graph*.

20 September. The *Daily Express* reports that ATV ha
paid £1,000,000 "for just enough shares to give i
near fifty per cent control of The Beatles' music
publishing company Northern Songs," adding tha
McCartney is the biggest Beatle holder with 751,
000 shares worth £1,500,000 at the ATV price
and that John Lennon has 694,000 shares wort
£1,400,000, and Ringo Starr 40,000 wort
£80,000. George Harrison had sold all his share
the previous year.

25 September. At the ATV annual general meeting, th
chairman Lord Renwick says ATV now owns 5
per cent of Northern Songs.

26 September. Apple releases The Beatles' "Abbey Road"
LP. Tracks: "Come Together," "I Want You
(She's So Heavy)," "Maxwell's Silver Hammer,"
"Sun King," "Because," "Something" (George
Harrison), "Polythene Pam," "Octopuses Garden"
(Ringo Starr), "You Never Give Me You
Money," "Mean Mr. Mustard," "Golden Slum-
bers," "Carry That Weight" and "Here Comes Th
Sun."

October. John Lennon and the Plastic Ono Band, with
Eric Clapton on guitar, release "Cold Turkey"/
"Don't Worry Kyoko" (Apple).

16 October. Announced that The Beatles are to sell all
their shares in Northern Songs to ATV at a price
"in accordance with the terms laid down by the
Take-over Panel."

22 October. With rumours sweeping the US that he is
dead, McCartney tells the *Evening Standard*: "I'm
dead, am I? Why does nobody ever tell me anything?"

9 November. John and Yoko reported to have made a
film of themselves floating through clouds over
Hampshire in a hot air balloon. The film is called
"Apotheosis."

23 November. Lennon returns his MBE as a protest
against British support of the US in Vietnam,
British policy towards the war in Biafra, and "Cold
Turkey" slipping down the charts.

December. The *Sunday Express* reports that all Apple
staff—just like those of the Royal Family—now
have to sign an undertaking never to write about
their employers.

December. John Lennon releases the "Live Peace in Toronto" LP, with Eric Clapton on guitar.

8 December. The *Daily Express* reports that The Beatles
have now filed company reports for the 18 months
ended December, 1966, showing profits of
£574,000—compared with profits of £519,000
in the previous twelve months.

11 December. US promoter Mike Belkin offers The
Beatles a minimum of 2,400,000 US dollars for a
12-city tour plus 65 per cent of the gross which he
estimates would earn them another 6,400,000 dollars. They turn it down.

1970

17 January. Apple group Badfinger enters the *New Musical Express* chart with "Come and Get It," a song

written by Paul McCartney which they feature in the film "The Magic Christian."

21 January. Reported in the *Daily Express* that John Lennon had turned skinhead. "We can travel unrecognised," he says.

February. John Lennon and the Plastic Ono Band release "Instant Karma"/"Who Has Seen The Wind" (Yoko Ono). Produced by Phil Spector (Apple).

March. Lennon's exhibition of lithographs showing his love-making positions with Yoko Ono seized at a London art gallery on grounds of indecency.

April. Paul McCartney releases his first solo LP "McCartney." Tracks: "The Lovely Linda," "That Would Be Something," "Valentine Day," "Every Night," "Hot As Sun," "Glasses," "Junk," "Man We Was Lonely," "Oo You," "Momma Miss America," "Teddy Boy," "Singalong Junk," "Maybe I'm Amazed" and "Kreen-Akrore" (Apple).

2 April. Paul tells the *Evening Standard*: "We all have to ask each other's permission before any of us does anything without the other three. My own record nearly didn't come out because Klein and some of the others thought it would be too near to the date of the next Beatles album . . . I had to get George, who's a director of Apple, to authorise its release for me . . . we're all talking about peace and love but really we're not feeling peaceful at all."

Ringo Starr releases his own solo LP "Sentimental Journey."

9 April. Paul McCartney appears in a five-minute London Weekend TV segment singing "Maybe I'm Amazed."

10 April. Announced that Paul McCartney has left The Beatles "because of personal, business and musical differences." Apple press officer, Derek Taylor says: "They do not want to split up, but the present rift seems to be part of their growing up . . . at the moment they seem to cramp each other's

styles. Paul has called a halt to The Beatles' activities. They could be dormant for years."

12 April. Reported in *New Musical Express* that Paul has formed a new company McCartney Productions Ltd., which has bought the film rights to the cartoon strip "Rupert The Bear" and is planning to produce and write all the music for a Rupert film.

17 April. Sir Lew Grade describes Paul McCartney's first album as "absolutely brilliant."

John Lennon tells *Rolling Stone*: "I'm telling you what's going on. It's John, George and Ringo as individuals. We're not even communicating with or making plans about Paul. We're just reacting to everything he does. It's a simple fact that he couldn't have his own way, so he's causing chaos . . . Paul was the same with Brian (Epstein) at the beginning. He used to sulk and God knows what. It's always been the same, only now it's bigger because we're all bigger."

8 May. The "Let It Be" LP released by Apple. One track "Dig It" was written by all four Beatles. Other tracks: "For You, Blue" (George Harrison), "Across The Universe," "Maggie May," "Let It Be," "The Long and Winding Road," "Two Of Us," "Dig A Pony," "I, Me My" (George Harrison), "I've Got A Feeling," "One after 909" and "Get Back." LP produced by Phil Spector.

13 May. The "Let It Be" film premiered in New York.

20 May. The "Let It Be" film premiered simultaneously in London and Liverpool—but none of The Beatles turn up.

23 May. Reported in the US that the "Let It Be" LP had advance orders of 3,700,000—worth 25,900,000 US dollars—the largest initial sale in the history of the US record industry. When one track "Long and Winding Road" was released as a single it also sold 1,200,000 copies within two days. The "McCartney" solo LP had also sold over 1,000,-000 copies in four weeks, and Ringo's "Sentimen-

tal Journey" LP had grossed 500,000 in two weeks (*New Musical Express*).

27 June. Reported that a good quality stereo bootleg LP of The Beatles was on sale in London titled "Get Back to Toronto." Includes some conversation plus "Let It Be," "Peace Message—Get Back," "Teddy Boy," "On Our Way Back Home," "All I Want Is You," "Get Back" (again), "I Got A Feeling," "Don't Let Me Down," "Sweet and Lovely Girl," "When You Walk" (Christmas message).

1 August. Cynthia Lennon marries Italian hotelier Roberto Bassanini at Kensington register office—with Julian as page boy. Only show business people present were Twiggy and Justin de Villeneuve.

September. Ringo Starr's second solo album "Beaucoup of Blues" and George Harrison's triple set "All Things Must Pass" released by Apple.

December. John Lennon's Plastic Ono Band album released (Apple).

31 December. Paul McCartney starts High Court proceedings to end The Beatles' partnership. He issues a writ seeking a declaration that the partnership "The Beatles & Co." formed in April, 1967, ought to be dissolved and accordingly be dissolved, that its affairs be wound up, and that a Receiver be appointed.

1971

9 January. George Harrison at No. 1 in the US singles chart with "My Sweet Lord" and at No. 1 in the LP charts with the triple set "All Things Must Pass."

9 January. Reported that Paul McCartney had bought another 400 acres of land next to his farm, High Park, near Campbeltown.

18 February. Paul and Linda McCartney attend High Court, hearing counsel say that Allen Klein's company had drawn about £1,500,000 commission from the group. Court also told that in 1970 The Beatles had an income of approximately £4,000,-

180

000. Later the Court was told by Mr. Morris Finer, QC, appearing for John, George, Ringo and Apple Corps Ltd., who were all opposing McCartney's application, that when Klein took over in 1969 the group were verging on bankruptcy—and he tried very successfully to get them out of this "dreadful mess" by generating income as soon as possible.

25 February. Evidence by Allen Klein read to the High Court, stating that The Beatles earned more than £17,500,000 in the eight and a half years to December, 1970 and that £9,000,000 of that had been earned in the previous 19 months. The Court was told that this income did not include songwriting income.

February. Paul McCartney releases "Another Day," co-written with his wife Linda (Apple). The *Evening Standard* reports that "half the copyright is being claimed by Maclen Music Ltd. (the first assignees of copyright of all Lennon and McCartney compositions), and the other half by a company called McCartney Inc.

5 March. John Lennon and the Plastic Ono Band release "Power To The People"/"Open Your Box" (Yoko and the Plastic Ono Band) (Apple).

10 March. In the High Court, a Receiver (Mr. J. D. Spooner) is appointed to handle The Beatles' assets, and Allen Klein is prevented from further management of the group's affairs. Mr. Justice Stamp says: "A Receiver, in my judgement, is needed so that there may be a firm hand to produce order. I have no doubt that a Receiver and Manager ought to be appointed."

17 March. Paul McCartney at No. 1 in the *New Musical Express* chart with "Another Day"/"Woman Oh Why" (Apple).

12 May. Paul and Linda McCartney with their children together with Ringo and Maureen Starr go to St. Tropez for Mick Jagger's wedding to Bianca. Announced that Ringo Starr is to film a Western

"Blindman" on location in Italy and Spain, playing a vicious bandit.

21 May. Paul and Linda McCartney release "Ram" LP (Apple). Cover photos by Linda of Paul holding a ram by the horns outside their home in Scotland. Tracks: "Too Many People," "Three Legs," "Ram On," "Dear Boy," Uncle Albert," "Admiral Halsey," "Smile Away," "Heart of the Country," "Monkberry Moon Delight," "Eat At Home," "Long Haired Lady," "Ram On" (reprise) and "Back Seat of my Car." Paul says: "Linda was very present all the way through. We've been writing many more songs together and we're developing as a harmony team . . . I found this New York drummer named Denny and we just went to work the following Monday." Paul and Linda McCartney release a single "Back Seat Of My Car"/ "Heart Of The Country" (Apple).

31 July. Lennon tells the *New Musical Express*: "The thing with Paul is he wants all the action. He wants it all. It's not just the money. It's the principle. I think, for instance, that Paul's cost us probably over a million since he started this thing . . . it's like Monopoly, only with real money . . . and costing us a fortune."

1 August. The Bangla Desh Concert at Madison Square Garden with George Harrison, Ringo Starr, Bob Dylan, Badfinger, Leon Russell, Eric Clapton, Ravi Shankar and Billy Preston—which raises 255,971 dollars for relief in Bangla Desh even before record royalties are assessed.

August. John and Yoko settle in New York.

September. John Lennon releases his "Imagine" LP.

18 September. Although "Uncle Albert"/"Admiral Halsey" is released as a US single, McCartney decides not to release the single in Britain as he "does not want to keep selling the past."

December. Paul McCartney releases his "Wings Wild Life" LP (Apple). Tracks: "Bip Bop," "Love Is Strange," "Wild Life," "Some People Never

Know," "I Am Your Singer," "Tomorrow" and Dear Friend." Denny Laine is now a member of Wings.

December. John Lennon releases "Happy Xmas (War Is Over)," recorded by John and Yoko with the Plastic Ono Band and the Harlem Community Choir.

1972

28 January. After five years Decca re-release "Say You Don't Mind"/"Ask The People" by Denny Laine.

30 January. Newly recruited member of Wings Henry McCullough talks to the *New Musical Express*.

February. The BBC ban Paul McCartney and Wings' single "Give Ireland Back to the Irish" (Parts I and 2) (Apple).

8 February. Paul and Wings arrive at Nottingham University to ask if Wings can play there next day— his first live appearance in over five years.

9 February. Paul and Wings play at the University to an audience of 700 students.

14 February. John and Yoko begin a week co-hosting "The Mike Douglas Show" on New York TV, playing on one session with Chuck Berry.

26 February. Linda McCartney tells *Melody Maker*: "Eric Clapton once said that he would like to play from the back of a caravan, but he never got around to doing it. Well we have! We've no manager or agents—just we five and the roadies. We're just a gang of musicians touring around."

29 February. John Lennon's US non immigrant visa expires—but he stays on in New York because of the search for Yoko's child Kyoko, who is with her father. The Government refuses to extend his authorisation to stay and his battle with the immigration authorities begins.

29 April. John Lindsay, Mayor of New York, asks the Federal authorities to allow John and Yoko to remain permanently in America and to quash the deportation proceedings. "A grave injustice is being perpetrated," he says.

30 April. John and Yoko release the jointly written single "Woman Is The Nigger of the World," with the B-side written and sung by Yoko, "Sister Oh Sister." Both are tracks from the LP "Some Time In New York City," also released at this time. The backing is by the Plastic Ono Band and Elephants Memory. The LP was a double record set—the other record featuring extracts from a 1969 concert at the Lyceum with the Lennons, George Harrison, Eric Clapton, Keith Moon and Delaney and Bonnie on one side, and on the other extracts from a concert at Fillmore East when John and Yoko jammed with Frank Zappa.

May. Paul McCartney and Wings release "Mary Had A Little Lamb"/"Little Woman Love" (Apple).

9 July. Paul McCartney and Wings begin seven week European tour at Château Vallon Centre Culturelle.

12 July. Juan Les Pins.

13 July. Arles Theatre Antique.

14 July. Lyons.

16 July. Paris Olympia.

18 July. Munich Circus Krone.

19 July. Frankfurt Offenbach Hall.

21 July. Zurich Congress Halle.

22 July. Montreux Pavilion, and then a few days' rest.

1 August. Copenhagen KB Hall.

4 August. Helsinki Maess Hall.

5 August. Turku Idraets (Finland).

7 August. Stockholm Tivoli Gardens.

8 August. Oerebro Idretis Hall (Sweden).

9 August. Oslo.

10 August. Gothenburg Scandinavian.

11 August. Lund Olympean.

12 August. The *Daily Mirror* reports that Customs officials and police in Gothenburg "busted" Paul, Linda and Denny Seiwell who "confessed" to smoking cannabis sent to Wings daily by post from London. All three were ordered to pay £800, and the public prosecutor said formal charges would be brought later.

13 August. Odense Flyns Farum.

14 August. Aarhus Wejlby.

16 August. Hanover.

17 August. Gronnegan (Holland).

18 August. Rotterdam (Holland).

19 August. Breda (Holland).

20 August. Amsterdam (Holland).

22 August. Brussels.

24 August. Berlin Deutschland Halle.

23 October. Ringo Starr begins work on the film "That'll Be The Day" with David Essex, Keith Moon and Billy Fury.

1 December. Paul McCartney and Wings release "Hi, Hi, Hi," which is banned by BBC Radios One and Two. Press officer says: "We thought the record unfit for broadcasting because of the lyric." The coupling was "C Moon." Both titles were composed by Paul and Linda. It was released by Apple.

2 December. Paul tells *New Musical Express*: " 'Mary Had A Little Lamb' wasn't a great record, but the funny thing about that is we've got a whole new audience of eight year olds and five-to-six year olds—like Pete Townshend's daughter."

1973

March. In New York, the US Immigration Department orders John Lennon's deportation because of his 1968 drugs conviction.

8 March. Paul McCartney fined £100 at Campbeltown for growing cannabis at his farm. "I must admit I did expect it to be worse," he says afterwards. His counsel says the plants had been grown from seeds sent through the post by a fan. Afterwards Paul and Linda hire a jet and fly back to London.

18 March. Paul and Linda appear with Wings at the Hard Rock cafe, London, raising funds for Release, the charity that helps drug-takers and other young people in trouble.

23 March. Paul McCartney and Wings release "My Love"/ "The Mess" (Apple).

16 April. The "James Paul McCartney" ATV special screened in the US, described as "a personal project of Sir Lew Grade, realised through the genius of Paul McCartney and the expertise of producer Gary Smith and director Dwight Hewison."

21 April. Henry McCullough tells *Melody Maker*: "I don't suppose we'll be together for ever. I'm sure Paul's got more of a tie to The Beatles than to Wings . . . Wings has all the makings of a great group, but our battle is to keep it as a band and not let it fall apart as it could so easily do."

Paul McCartney and Wings release the "Red Rose Speedway" LP. Tracks: "Big Barn Red," "My Love," "Get On The Right Thing," "One More Kiss," "Little Lamb Dragonfly," "Single Pigeon," "When The Night," "Loup (First Indian On The Moon)," medley of "Hold Me Tight," "Lazy Dynamite," "Hands of Love" and "Power Cut" (Apple).

10 May. The "James Paul McCartney" ATV special shown in Britain.

11 May. Paul McCartney and Wings begin their first major British tour—the first scheduled tour by an ex-Beatle since their last appearance together in 1966. First concert is at Bristol Hippodrome.

12 May. Oxford New Theatre.

13 May. Cardiff Capitol.

15 May. Bournemouth Winter Gardens.

16 May. Manchester Hard Rock.

17 May. Manchester Hard Rock.

18 May. Liverpool Empire (two concerts).

19 May. Leeds University.

21 May. Preston Guildhall.

23 May. Edinburgh Odeon.

24 May. Glasgow Green's Playhouse.

25 May. Hammersmith Odeon.

26 May. Hammersmith Odeon.

27 May. Hammersmith Odeon (a third concert specially

arranged because of an overwhelming demand for tickets).

1 June. Wings' theme song from the James Bond film "Live and Let Die" released by Apple. McCartney wrote the song.

4 July. Wings agree to visit some of the cities missed on the first tour—starting at Sheffield City Hall.

5 July. Stoke Trentham Gardens, and also attend James Bond film "Live and Let Die" premiere at Leicester Square Odeon.

6 July. Birmingham Odeon.

9 July. Leicester Odeon.

10 July. Newcastle City Hall.

11 July. McCartney tells *Melody Maker*: "The way we tour now, it seems easier. It's not actually more organised, but we get days off every now and then, so it's quite good. It hasn't ground me into the ground, anyway."

23 September. Paul and Linda McCartney arrive back at Gatwick Airport after six weeks in Lagos, Nigeria, recording tracks, including their "Band On The Run" LP. (Only the three of them went out there; Henry McCullough and Denny Seiwell left Wings shortly before their planned departure—leaving just Paul, Linda and Denny Laine.)

October. Paul McCartney and Wings release "Helen Wheels"/"Country Dreamer" (Apple).

19 October. Ringo Starr releases the single "Photograph"/ "Down and Out" (Apple).

27 October. The *Melody Maker* reports that Paul McCartney is writing the music for a 90-minute Twiggy TV special "Gotta Sing, Gotta Dance."

November. John Lennon releases his "Mind Games" LP (Apple).

30 November. Denny Laine's solo LP "Ahh Laine" released on the Wizard label, produced by Denny and Ian Horne, roadie with Wings.

December. Paul McCartney and Wings release the "Band On The Run" LP. Other tracks: "Blue Bird," "Jet," "Let Me Roll It," "Marmunia," "No

Words," "Drink To Me" and "Nineteen Eighty Five" (Apple).

11 December. Reported in the *Evening Standard* that John Lennon has given £1,000 to help the ailing "underground" magazine *International Times*. Ringo releases his "Ringo" LP, on which all former Beatles worked in some way. McCartney wrote the track "Six O'Clock." (Apple.)

1974

18 February. Paul McCartney and Wings release "Jet"/ "Let Me Roll It" (Apple).

25 February. In the High Court, Judge Megarry approves a scheme to help the Receiver carry on running the Beatles' partnership affairs. Paul tells the *Daily Mail*: "As soon as things are sorted out we can all get together again and do something. We've talked about it, but haven't been able to do anything because this has been going on and on."

13 April. Reported that Jane Asher had given birth to a baby girl at Middlesex Hospital, where staff "were given strict instructions by the actress not to release details."

25 May. Reported that George Harrison had formed his own record label Dark Horse Records, and had signed a world-wide distribution deal in Paris with A & M Records.

June/August. Paul and Linda McCartney spend seven weeks recording in Nashville with Denny Laine and the new members of Wings Jimmy McCulloch and Geoff Britton.

14 June. Reported that "Band On The Run" as well as being No. 1 in the US has also reached No. 1 in Australia, Norway and Sweden earning a Gold Disc in each country.

18 June. McCartney tells the *Daily Express*: "I've discovered I'm rather old-fashioned. I believe in the marriage contract."

28 June. Paul McCartney and Wings release the title track from "Band on the Run," coupled with "Zoo

Gang"—and full page photo advertisements in the music press show them receiving 14 gold discs for the LP's successes world-wide.

4 July. John Christie releases "July 4," written by Paul and Linda McCartney and produced by Dave Clark (Polydor).

24 July. Denny Laine tells the *Evening News* that his relationship with McCartney is based on trust: "I have signed so many contracts that have got me into so much trouble that I never want to sign anything again."

26 July. Three-day Beatles Appreciation Convention opens in Boston—and two months later another "Beatlefest '74" is staged in New York.

14 August. Reported that a bronze sculpture of The Beatles—one of twelve offered by sculptor David Wynne for £1,500 each in 1964—is now being offered for sale at £35,000.

15 August. "John, Paul, George, Ringo and Bert" opens at the Lyric Theatre, London, written by Liverpool schoolmaster Willy Russell, and originally presented at the Everyman's Theatre, Liverpool.

16 August. Reported in the *Daily Mail* that Lennon and McCartney have both signed co-publishing agreements with ATV Music which "will bolster Lennon's bank account by a sum in excess of £1,000,000 . . ."

Adam Faith brings out the LP "I Survive" (Warner Brothers) on which Paul and Linda McCartney are featured.

31 August. Lennon claims in the US Federal Court that the Nixon administration tried to have him deported because they had heard he was one of the organisers of an anti-war demonstration at the Republican Convention in San Diego in 1972; John also says his phone was tapped. Of his 1968 cannabis conviction John says after the hearing: "I thought it would just go away, it'd be like a parking fine, you know. I was living with Yoko and she was

pregnant. And I thought they'd let her off if I pleaded guilty."

6 September. George Harrison launches his own record label, Dark Horse, with "The Place I Love" LP by Splinter. Jonathan Clyde becomes a director of Dark Horse, who later release the Splinter single "Costa Fine Town."

13 September. Harry Nilsson releases "Many Rivers To Cross," arranged and produced by John Lennon, taken from the LP "Pussy Cats" on which they worked together.

20 September. Polydor announce that they will be distributing records released on Ringo Starr's new label Ring O'Records.

23 September. Ravi Shankar Music Festival at the Royal Albert Hall, London, produced by George Harrison.

4 October. John Lennon releases his LP "Walls and Bridges" (Apple), and the single "Whatever Gets You Thru The Night," on which Elton John plays organ and piano.

5 October. Mike McGear's solo LP "McGear" released by Warner Brothers, with Wings playing on the backing tracks, and Paul McCartney producing.

12 October. John Lennon tells *New Musical Express*: "When we see each other, there's no tension. We get on fine . . . but I'm sure if we ever did anything it would be in 1976, when the contract runs out . . . together we would sound exactly the same, only better—cos we're all better now, y'know."

25 October. Wings release "Junior's Farm"/"Sally G.," both written and recorded in Nashville. The Country Hams release "Walking In The Park With Eloise," recorded by a group of Nashville musicians. The song was written by Paul's father, and the recording produced by Paul.

At an American press conference George Harrison says of his wife Patti, now living with Eric Clapton: "Eric Clapton's been a close friend for years.

I'm very happy about it. I'm still very friendly with him . . . he's great. I'd rather she was with him than with some dope."

2 November. George Harrison begins a US tour in Vancouver, playing fifty concerts in 27 cities over a period of seven weeks—accompanied by Tom Horn, Chuck Findlay, Andy Newmark, Emil Richards, Tom Scott, Robben Ford, Billy Preston and Willie Weeks.

4 November. "Sgt. Pepper's Lonely Hearts Club Band On The Road" stage show opens in Hartford, Connecticut.

November. Paul McCartney and Wings spend November recording in London, and then January and February (1975) recording in New Orleans.

November. Ringo Starr's "Goodnight Vienna" LP released (Apple). The title track was written by John Lennon.

John Lennon featured on Elton John's version of "Lucy In The Sky with Diamonds."

18 November. Paul and Linda join Rod Stewart and The Faces on stage at Lewisham Odeon to sing "Mine for Me," one of Paul's songs which The Faces regularly feature.

21 November. Wings appear on "Top Of The Pops" (BBC-1) to promote "Junior's Farm," and also appear backing David Essex's vocals on "Gonna Make You A Star."

28 November. John Lennon joins Elton John on stage at Madison Square Garden, New York to sing "Whatever Gets You Thru The Night," "Lucy In The Sky With Diamonds" and "I Saw Her Standing There."

6 December. George Harrison releases his "Dark Horse" LP (Apple), and his single "Ding Dong" (Apple).

13 December. George Harrison and his father Harry visit the White House, Washington, and says he senses "good vibes" coming from President Ford's administration. The Harrisons are invited there for lunch

by the President's son John whom they met on tour.

14 December. George Harrison withdraws permission for his song "Here Comes The Sun" to be used in the London stage show "John, Paul, George, Ringo and Bert"—and it is replaced by the Lennon and McCartney number "Good Day Sunshine."

16 December. The *Daily Mail* reports that "a secret and near hysterical" White House report lies behind Lennon's dispute with the US immigration authorities, and that former President Nixon "personally ordered Government officials to harass Lennon and kick him out of America . . ."

20 December. George Harrison's US tour ends at Madison Square Garden, New York.

21 December. Full page advertisements in the music papers to announce that Paul McCartney and Wings have been awarded a platinum disc for over 500,-000 sales in Britain of the "Band On The Run" LP.